DIGITAL MINIMALISM

HOW TO DISCONNECT FOR A BETTER LIFE

DAVID SANDUA

Digital Minimalism. How to disconnect for a better life.

"We don't need more technology to be more connected.
We need more humanity."

Maxime Lagacé

INDEX

9

10

11

I. INTRODUCTION

In today's hyperconnected world, the constant presence of technology can feel overwhelming, leading to an increase in stress, anxiety, and decreased productivity. This is where the concept of digital minimalism comes into play. It is a philosophy that advocates for intentionally reducing the time spent on digital devices and focusing instead on meaningful, offline activities. By disconnecting from the endless notifications and distractions that come with digital technology, individuals can regain control over their time and attention. Digital minimalism encourages a more mindful and deliberate approach to technology use, allowing for a clearer mind and increased productivity. In this essay, we will explore the principles of digital minimalism and how implementing them can lead to a better, more balanced life in our digital age.

Definition of digital minimalism

Digital minimalism can be defined as a philosophy of technology use that focuses on intentionally reducing the time spent on digital devices and platforms to prioritize activities that add value to one's life. This concept emphasizes the importance of being mindful of how technology is integrated into daily routines, promoting a more intentional and meaningful use of digital tools. By cutting out unnecessary distractions and decluttering digital spaces, individuals can create a healthier balance between the virtual and real worlds, leading to increased productivity, improved mental well-being, and deeper connections with others. Digital minimalism encourages individuals to curate their digital lives, opting for quality over quantity when it comes to online interactions and content consumption. Ultimately, this approach seeks to help individuals cultivate a more focused and fulfilling existence in a digitized world.

Importance of digital minimalism in modern life

In the fast-paced digital world we live in today, the concept of digital minimalism has become increasingly important for individuals seeking a healthier and more balanced lifestyle. By practicing digital minimalism, one can disconnect from the constant distractions of technology and focus on what truly matters. This approach allows for more intentional and mindful use of digital tools, leading to increased productivity, improved mental health, and stronger relationships. Digital minimalism encourages individuals to prioritize their time and energy on activities that bring value and fulfillment, rather than being constantly tethered to screens and devices. In a society where technology is ever-present, embracing digital minimalism can help individuals regain control over their attention and time, ultimately leading to a more meaningful and fulfilling life.

Overview of the essay structure

The structure of this essay on digital minimalism begins with an introduction that defines the concept and its significance in today's hyper-connected world. This sets the stage for the subsequent exploration of the benefits of disconnecting from digital distractions and reclaiming control over our attention. The body of the essay is divided into sections that delve into the practical strategies and techniques that individuals can implement to achieve digital minimalism in their own lives. These include setting boundaries with technology, engaging in digital decluttering, and cultivating offline hobbies and activities. Each section is supported by research and examples that illustrate the effectiveness of these practices in promoting mental well-being and enhancing productivity. The conclusion of the essay reinforces the importance of digital minimalism as a means of fostering a more balanced and fulfilling lifestyle in an increasingly digital age.

II. THE CONCEPT OF DIGITAL MINIMALISM

In the fast-paced digital age we live in, the concept of digital minimalism has emerged as a response to the overwhelming presence of technology in our lives. Digital minimalism encourages individuals to carefully curate their digital consumption, focusing on quality over quantity. By intentionally limiting the time spent on digital devices and platforms, individuals can reclaim their autonomy and prioritize meaningful real-world experiences. This intentional disconnect from the constant barrage of information and notifications allows for a more mindful approach to technology use, fostering a sense of calm and focus in an otherwise chaotic digital landscape. Embracing digital minimalism can also lead to increased productivity, better mental health, and enhanced relationships as individuals are able to allocate their time and attention to what truly matters. Overall, the concept of digital minimalism offers a compelling framework for finding balance and tranquility in an increasingly tech-saturated world.

Origins and development of the concept

The concept of digital minimalism can be traced back to the rise of technology in the late 20th and early 21st centuries. As smartphones, social media, and constant connectivity became ubiquitous, individuals began to feel overwhelmed by the constant stream of information and notifications. This led to a growing awareness of the need to disconnect and find a healthier balance with technology. The development of the digital minimalism movement was fueled by the realization that excessive screen time and digital clutter were negatively impacting mental health, relationships, and overall well-being. As a response to this digital overload, thought leaders and scholars began to advocate for strategies to simplify and declutter one's digital life. By emphasizing mindfulness, intentional technology use, and setting boundaries with devices, digital minimalism emerged as a powerful tool for individuals seeking a more deliberate and fulfilling relationship with technology.

Key principles of digital minimalism

Digital minimalism is based on several key principles that can help individuals achieve a healthier relationship with technology. One key principle is intentionality, which involves being deliberate and conscious about the ways in which technology is used in daily life. By setting clear boundaries and being mindful of how much time is spent on digital devices, individuals can regain control over their attention and focus. Another important principle is prioritization, which involves identifying the most valuable digital tools and activities and eliminating or reducing the rest. This allows individuals to allocate their time and energy towards activities that align with their values and goals. Finally, digital minimalism emphasizes quality over quantity, encouraging individuals to curate their digital lives by focusing on high-quality content and meaningful interactions rather than mindless scrolling and consumption. By embracing these principles, individuals can disconnect from the constant distractions of technology and cultivate a more intentional and fulfilling life.

Differences between digital minimalism and digital detox

One key distinction between digital minimalism and digital detox lies in their approaches to managing technology usage. Digital minimalism focuses on intentionally selecting the digital tools and platforms that offer the most value and eliminating the rest, encouraging a more mindful and purposeful relationship with technology. On the other hand, digital detox involves taking a temporary break from all digital devices and platforms to reset and recharge, often as a response to feeling overwhelmed or burnt out. While digital minimalism emphasizes the importance of making deliberate choices about technology usage to enhance productivity and well-being in the long term, digital detox is more about taking a short-term break as a form of self-care. Both concepts aim to reduce the negative effects of excessive screen time, but they differ in terms of the duration and intention behind the approach. Ultimately, understanding the nuances between digital minimalism and digital detox can help individuals adopt a more balanced and sustainable relationship with technology.

III. THE PREVALENCE OF DIGITAL OVERLOAD

In today's fast-paced digital age, the prevalence of digital overload has become a pressing concern for many individuals. With constant notifications, emails, social media updates, and the temptation of endless scrolling, it can be challenging to disconnect and find a sense of balance. The allure of constant connectivity can lead to feelings of overwhelm, anxiety, and even a sense of addiction to our devices. As we become increasingly reliant on technology for work, social connection, and entertainment, it is crucial to recognize the negative impact of digital overload on our mental health and overall well-being. Implementing principles of digital minimalism, such as setting boundaries with technology use, decluttering digital spaces, and prioritizing real-world experiences, can help individuals reclaim their time and attention, leading to a more intentional and fulfilling life. By addressing the prevalence of digital overload, we can work towards creating a healthier relationship with technology and achieving a greater sense of balance in our daily lives.

Statistics on digital usage globally

Digital usage globally is on a steady rise, with statistics revealing the extent to which technology has become ingrained in our daily lives. According to recent data, there are over 4.57 billion active internet users worldwide, representing a significant portion of the global population. This number is expected to grow even further in the coming years as access to technology becomes more widespread. Furthermore, mobile phone usage continues to dominate the digital landscape, with over 5.21 billion unique mobile phone users globally. These figures highlight the pervasive influence of digital technology and the constant connectivity it offers. While the benefits of digital connectivity are undeniable, it is essential to recognize the potential drawbacks of excessive digital usage, such as decreased productivity, mental health issues, and reduced face-to-face interactions. By understanding the current statistics on digital usage globally, individuals can make informed decisions about their own digital consumption and strive to achieve a more balanced and mindful approach to technology use.

Psychological effects of excessive digital consumption

It is evident that excessive digital consumption can have profound psychological effects on individuals. Constant exposure to social media, online gaming, and other digital platforms can lead to feelings of anxiety, depression, and a sense of isolation. The constant barrage of information and notifications can overwhelm the mind, leading to decreased attention span and difficulty focusing on tasks. Moreover, the comparison culture perpetuated on social media can result in feelings of inadequacy and low self-esteem. Research has also shown a link between excessive screen time and poor sleep quality, further exacerbating mental health issues. To combat these negative effects, embracing digital minimalism can be a beneficial approach. By intentionally reducing screen time and focusing on real-life interactions and activities, individuals can regain control over their mental well-being and cultivate a more balanced and fulfilling life.

Social implications of a digitally overloaded society

In a digitally overloaded society, the social implications are vast and significant. One major consequence is the breakdown of face-to-face communication and human connection. With the prevalence of screens and devices, people often opt for virtual interactions over real-life conversations, leading to a decline in empathy and emotional intelligence. Additionally, the constant bombardment of information can result in heightened levels of stress and anxiety, as individuals feel the pressure to keep up with the digital world at all times. This obsession with technology can also lead to a decrease in productivity and overall well-being, as people find themselves constantly distracted and unable to focus on meaningful tasks. Overall, the impact of living in a digitally saturated environment can be detrimental to our social fabric, highlighting the urgent need for individuals to embrace digital minimalism and reclaim control over their lives.

IV. PSYCHOLOGICAL IMPACT OF DIGITAL OVERLOAD

Psychological Impact of Digital Overload can have profound effects on our mental well-being. As individuals immerse themselves in a constant stream of digital content, they may experience heightened levels of stress, anxiety, and even depression. The pressure to stay connected, respond to messages, and keep up with social media can lead to burnout and feelings of inadequacy. The endless scrolling and constant notifications disrupt our focus and ability to concentrate, leading to decreased productivity and cognitive overload. Moreover, the comparison trap fostered by social media platforms can erode self-esteem and contribute to feelings of isolation. Digital overload can also negatively impact our sleep patterns, as the blue light emitted by screens interferes with our circadian rhythms. By practicing digital minimalism and setting boundaries on our use of technology, we can reclaim our mental clarity and create a healthier relationship with the digital world.

Impact on attention span and memory

In today's digital age, the constant bombardment of information and distractions from technology has a significant impact on our attention span and memory. With the endless notifications, emails, and social media alerts vying for our attention, it becomes increasingly challenging to focus on one task for an extended period. This continuous multitasking and quick switching between tasks can lead to a decrease in our ability to concentrate deeply on any one thing, ultimately affecting our attention span. Additionally, the reliance on digital devices for storing information can hinder our memory retention. When we rely on external sources such as smartphones or the internet to remember information, our brains don't have the opportunity to encode and retain that information effectively. By practicing digital minimalism and disconnecting from unnecessary technology, individuals can regain control over their attention span and memory, leading to improved focus and cognitive abilities.

Relationship between digital overload and stress levels

Digital overload has been closely linked to increased stress levels in individuals. The constant bombardment of notifications, emails, and social media updates can lead to feelings of overwhelm and anxiety. As people spend more time glued to their screens, they often neglect real-life interactions and self-care activities, further exacerbating their stress levels. Research has shown that excessive screen time can disrupt sleep patterns, as the blue light emitted by devices interferes with the production of melatonin, a hormone essential for sleep. Moreover, the pressure to constantly stay connected and responsive in a digital world can contribute to a sense of being always "on," never truly able to disconnect and unwind. By embracing digital minimalism and setting boundaries on screen time, individuals can lessen the stimuli that contribute to stress and improve their overall well-being. Disconnecting from the digital world can create space for genuine connections, mindfulness, and relaxation, ultimately leading to a healthier and more balanced lifestyle.

Digital overload and its effects on sleep patterns

In today's hyper-connected world, the prevalence of digital devices has led to a phenomenon known as digital overload, which can have significant effects on sleep patterns. The constant exposure to screens emitting blue light before bedtime can disrupt the body's natural circadian rhythm, making it difficult to fall asleep and stay asleep. Moreover, the endless stream of notifications and alerts from smartphones and other devices can create a state of constant alertness, preventing the mind from unwinding and preparing for rest. Studies have shown that excessive screen time before bed is strongly associated with poor sleep quality and decreased overall sleep duration. To combat the negative impact of digital overload on sleep patterns, it is essential to practice digital minimalism by setting boundaries on screen time, turning off devices at least an hour before bedtime, and creating a calming bedtime routine to promote better sleep hygiene. By prioritizing quality rest over digital distractions, individuals can improve their sleep patterns and overall well-being.

V. DIGITAL MINIMALISM AND MENTAL HEALTH

In today's fast-paced digital age, the concept of digital minimalism has emerged as a powerful tool for promoting mental health and overall well-being. By intentionally reducing the time spent on digital devices and online platforms, individuals can create space for meaningful real-life interactions, hobbies, and activities that promote mental clarity and emotional balance. This intentional disconnection allows individuals to break free from the constant distractions and notifications that can contribute to feelings of anxiety, stress, and overwhelm. By curating a more intentional and purposeful relationship with technology, individuals can experience improved focus, increased mindfulness, and greater satisfaction in their daily lives. Digital minimalism empowers individuals to take control of their technology usage, leading to a healthier relationship with digital devices and a more balanced approach to navigating the digital landscape. Ultimately, the practice of digital minimalism serves as a valuable tool for cultivating a more peaceful and fulfilling mental state amidst the noise of the digital world.

Enhancing focus and reducing anxiety

Furthermore, digital minimalism is not just about reducing distractions; it also has a significant impact on enhancing focus and reducing anxiety. By disconnecting from the constant barrage of notifications and social media updates, individuals can create a more serene mental environment that allows for deep concentration and mindfulness. Studies have shown that excessive screen time can lead to increased levels of stress and anxiety, as the brain becomes overwhelmed by the endless stream of information. When we limit our digital consumption, we give ourselves the opportunity to tune into our thoughts and emotions, ultimately improving our ability to focus on the task at hand. This intentional disconnection from our devices can be a powerful tool in combating the mental fatigue and restlessness that often accompany our overly connected lifestyles. In this way, digital minimalism not only declutters our digital space but also declutters our minds, promoting a sense of calmness and clarity that is essential for overall well-being.

Benefits for depression and loneliness

In addition to improving productivity and focus, digital minimalism also offers significant benefits for mental health, particularly in combating feelings of depression and loneliness. By reducing the amount of time spent on social media and digital devices, individuals can nurture real-life connections and engage in more meaningful interactions, leading to a sense of belonging and fulfillment. Constant exposure to curated online personas and unrealistic standards can exacerbate feelings of inadequacy and isolation, contributing to symptoms of depression. Disconnecting from the digital world allows individuals to reconnect with themselves and others on a deeper level, fostering genuine relationships and improving overall well-being. Furthermore, the act of disconnecting can provide a much-needed mental break, promoting mindfulness and reducing stress. Embracing digital minimalism can be a powerful tool in combating the pervasive feelings of loneliness and depression that many individuals experience in our hyperconnected world.

Case studies of improved mental health through digital minimalism

It is evident through various case studies that adopting digital minimalism can lead to improved mental health outcomes. For instance, a study conducted by researchers at Stanford University found that participants who limited their use of social media and digital devices reported lower levels of stress, anxiety, and depression. By reducing the constant stream of information and notifications, individuals were able to focus more on meaningful interactions and activities that promoted well-being. In another case, a corporate professional struggling with burnout and insomnia implemented digital minimalism techniques, such as setting boundaries for phone usage and practicing mindfulness. As a result, he experienced improved sleep quality, reduced stress levels, and a newfound sense of calm and clarity. These real-life examples underscore the transformative power of disconnecting from the digital world and prioritizing mental health and self-care.

VI. DIGITAL MINIMALISM IN THE WORKPLACE

One key aspect of embracing digital minimalism in the workplace is the recognition that constant connectivity does not always equate to increased productivity. While it may seem that being constantly plugged in allows for quicker responses and seamless communication, the reality is that it often leads to distractions and a lack of focus on important tasks. By implementing strategies to limit digital distractions, such as turning off notifications, setting designated times for checking emails, and using software to block time-wasting websites, employees can create a more conducive work environment that fosters deep work and sustained attention. This intentional approach to technology use not only enhances productivity but also helps reduce stress and improve overall well-being in the workplace. Digital minimalism in the workplace is not about completely cutting off all technology, but rather about finding a healthy balance that allows for efficient work while also promoting mental clarity and focus.

Increasing productivity and efficiency

In the pursuit of increasing productivity and efficiency, the concept of digital minimalism offers a valuable framework for individuals seeking to optimize their daily routines. By deliberately reducing the digital distractions that often consume our time and attention, individuals are able to focus on tasks with greater clarity and purpose. This intentional disconnection from constant notifications and information overload allows for deeper engagement with work or activities, leading to improved efficiency and output. Moreover, by setting boundaries around technology use, individuals can create dedicated spaces for concentration and creativity, fostering a more productive environment. In essence, digital minimalism not only streamlines our interactions with technology but also cultivates a mindful approach to our daily habits, ultimately enhancing our ability to accomplish tasks effectively and efficiently.

Reducing digital distractions at work

One effective strategy for reducing digital distractions at work is to establish clear boundaries between personal and professional technology use. By designating specific times or spaces for checking personal messages or browsing social media, individuals can create a more focused work environment. Additionally, implementing digital detox periods, where screens are turned off for a set amount of time each day, can help to break the cycle of constant connectivity. Another useful approach is to declutter digital spaces by organizing email inboxes, desktops, and online bookmarks. By streamlining digital environments, individuals can reduce visual clutter, making it easier to concentrate on tasks without being overwhelmed by unnecessary information. Ultimately, by implementing these strategies and embracing a more mindful approach to technology use, individuals can reclaim their time and attention, leading to increased productivity and greater well-being in the workplace.

Case studies of companies implementing digital minimalism

Companies such as Basecamp and Slack have been highlighted as case studies in implementing digital minimalism within their organizations. By encouraging their employees to limit their digital distractions and focus on deep, meaningful work, these companies have seen significant improvements in productivity and employee well-being. Basecamp, for example, has opted for a four-day workweek during the summer months, allowing employees to rejuvenate and disconnect from their screens. Slack has also prioritized mindful digital habits by implementing communication guidelines, such as designated quiet hours for uninterrupted work. Through these case studies, it is evident that digital minimalism can create a more balanced and efficient work environment, ultimately leading to higher levels of job satisfaction and overall success for companies. By learning from these examples, other organizations can begin to implement similar strategies to optimize their workplace dynamics and promote a healthier relationship with technology.

VII. DIGITAL MINIMALISM IN EDUCATION

As digital technologies continue to infiltrate various aspects of our lives, the realm of education is no exception. In the context of academia, digital minimalism can serve as a transformative approach to learning. By encouraging students and educators to critically assess their digital habits and prioritize quality over quantity, digital minimalism in education promotes deep engagement with course material and fosters meaningful interactions in the learning environment. This intentional disconnection from the constant barrage of notifications and distractions allows individuals to cultivate focused attention, enhance critical thinking skills, and promote overall well-being. Additionally, embracing digital minimalism in education can lead to a more balanced and intentional use of technology, creating space for face-to-face interactions, in-depth discussions, and immersive learning experiences that are essential for intellectual growth and development. Ultimately, integrating digital minimalism into educational settings can empower individuals to reclaim agency over their digital lives and cultivate a more mindful approach to learning and knowledge acquisition.

Effects on student focus and learning outcomes

As students navigate the increasingly digital landscape of education, the effects on their focus and learning outcomes become a critical concern. Embracing digital minimalism can offer a solution to the distractions that often hinder student focus. By intentionally curating their digital usage and limiting exposure to non-essential technology, students can create a more conducive learning environment. This heightened focus can lead to improved retention of information and deeper engagement with course material. Additionally, digital minimalism encourages students to prioritize meaningful interactions and experiences over mindless scrolling, which can ultimately lead to enhanced cognitive functioning and academic performance. By fostering a mindful approach to technology use, students can cultivate the necessary skills to navigate the digital world effectively while also reaping the benefits of a more focused and productive learning experience.

Implementing digital minimalism in educational settings

In educational settings, implementing digital minimalism can lead to numerous benefits for both students and teachers. By encouraging a more intentional use of technology, educators can foster deeper focus, enhance critical thinking skills, and promote a more engaged learning environment. Digital minimalism can help students combat distractions, such as social media and constant notifications, allowing them to concentrate better on their coursework. Moreover, by reducing screen time and promoting face-to-face interactions, educators can cultivate stronger relationships within the classroom and foster a sense of community among students. Emphasizing the importance of disconnecting from technology can also help individuals develop better self-regulation skills and improve overall well-being. By integrating digital minimalism into educational practices, schools can create a more mindful and intentional approach to technology use, ultimately enhancing the learning experience for all involved.

Impact on teacher-student interactions

One of the key impacts of digital minimalism on teacher-student interactions is the promotion of deeper connections and more meaningful engagements. By reducing the distractions and constant notifications that come with excessive technology use, teachers can foster a more focused and present environment in the classroom. This shift allows for increased opportunities for one-on-one interactions, personalized feedback, and in-depth discussions. Students are more likely to engage actively in the learning process when they feel that their teacher is fully present and attentive. Additionally, digital minimalism encourages teachers to prioritize face-to-face communication and interpersonal relationships, which are essential for building trust and rapport with students. Ultimately, by embracing a more intentional approach to technology use, teachers can create a more conducive environment for meaningful teacher-student interactions that promote learning and growth.

VIII. SOCIAL RELATIONSHIPS IN THE AGE OF DIGITAL MINIMALISM

In the age of digital minimalism, social relationships undergo a significant transformation as individuals prioritize meaningful connections over superficial interactions. By disconnecting from the constant barrage of notifications and distractions, people are able to cultivate deeper, more authentic relationships with those around them. As digital minimalists focus on quality over quantity in their social interactions, they are more present and engaged in their conversations, fostering genuine connections that bring a sense of fulfillment and belonging. This intentional approach to social relationships not only enhances interpersonal communication but also promotes overall well-being by reducing the feelings of loneliness and isolation that can result from excessive screen time. Embracing digital minimalism allows individuals to nurture meaningful relationships that enrich their lives and contribute to their emotional growth and happiness.

Changes in communication patterns

In the digital age, changes in communication patterns have significantly impacted how we interact with others. Social media platforms, instant messaging apps, and video conferencing tools have revolutionized the way we connect with people, breaking down traditional barriers of time and space. This shift has led to increased convenience and efficiency in communication, allowing for instant exchanges of information and ideas. However, this constant connectivity can also lead to information overload and a sense of always being "on." As a result, some individuals are turning to digital minimalism as a way to disconnect from the constant barrage of notifications and messages, seeking a more focused and intentional approach to communication. By setting boundaries and establishing tech-free zones in their lives, people are finding a better balance between virtual interactions and real-world connections, ultimately leading to improved mental well-being and productivity.

Deepening personal relationships

In today's digital age, deepening personal relationships has become increasingly challenging as screens and devices dominate our daily interactions. However, by embracing the principles of digital minimalism, individuals can reclaim valuable time and energy to invest in meaningful connections with others. By consciously limiting the use of technology, individuals can prioritize face-to-face interactions, fostering genuine and authentic relationships. This intentional approach allows for deeper conversations, increased empathy, and stronger emotional connections. In a society where superficial online interactions often prevail, practicing digital minimalism can help individuals break free from the constraints of virtual communication and cultivate more fulfilling relationships in the real world. By stepping away from screens and investing time and effort into nurturing personal connections, individuals can experience a greater sense of fulfillment, belonging, and intimacy in their relationships.

Community building offline

In the age of digital overload, the importance of community building offline cannot be overstated. When individuals disconnect from their screens and engage in face-to-face interactions, a sense of belonging and connection is fostered. Offline communities offer opportunities for genuine human connection, empathy, and support that are often lacking in the virtual realm. By participating in community events, joining clubs, or attending gatherings, individuals can develop meaningful relationships that provide emotional nourishment and a sense of purpose. These interactions also allow for the exchange of ideas, skills, and experiences, enriching the lives of all involved. In a society where digital devices often dominate our time and attention, nurturing offline relationships and building real-world communities is essential for maintaining our mental and emotional well-being. By prioritizing offline connections, individuals can create a more fulfilling and balanced life outside the confines of the digital world.

IX. DIGITAL MINIMALISM AND PERSONAL DEVELOPMENT

One of the key benefits of embracing digital minimalism is the positive impact it can have on personal development. By intentionally reducing the time and energy spent on digital distractions, individuals can create space for more meaningful activities that promote growth and self-improvement. This practice allows people to focus on cultivating real-life connections, pursuing hobbies, and engaging in activities that align with their values and goals. By disconnecting from the constant stream of notifications and information overload, individuals can regain control over their time and attention, leading to increased mindfulness and productivity. Digital minimalism not only encourages a healthier relationship with technology but also fosters a sense of fulfillment and purpose in one's daily life. This intentional approach to digital consumption can lead to greater self-awareness, improved mental well-being, and a stronger sense of personal agency.

Fostering creativity and innovation

As individuals strive to disconnect from the constant digital distractions that permeate their lives, fostering creativity and innovation becomes essential. By embracing digital minimalism, individuals can create space for deep thinking, allowing ideas to flourish and innovative solutions to emerge. Removing the clutter of constant notifications and mindless scrolling enables individuals to tap into their creative potential and think more critically about the world around them. In this digital age, it is easy to get caught up in the noise of social media and the constant need for validation, which can stifle creativity. However, by intentionally disconnecting and embracing simplicity, individuals can nurture their creativity and push the boundaries of what is possible. Ultimately, digital minimalism provides a pathway to fostering creativity and innovation by encouraging individuals to slow down, reflect, and engage with the world in a more meaningful way.

Encouraging self-reflection and mindfulness

In a world dominated by digital distractions, encouraging self-reflection and mindfulness is a crucial antidote to combat the adverse effects of constant connectivity. By taking the time to pause, reflect, and tune into our inner thoughts and emotions, individuals can gain clarity and perspective on their lives. Mindfulness practices, such as meditation or deep breathing exercises, can help cultivate a sense of presence and awareness, allowing individuals to detach from the digital noise and focus on the present moment. Self-reflection, on the other hand, enables individuals to evaluate their relationship with technology, identify habits that may be detrimental to their well-being, and make intentional choices about how they engage with digital devices. By fostering self-awareness and mindfulness, individuals can gain control over their digital consumption, reduce stress, and cultivate a more balanced and fulfilling life.

Personal stories of transformation through digital minimalism

Digital minimalism has empowered individuals to take control of their technology usage and achieve transformative personal growth. By adopting minimalist principles, many have found themselves breaking free from the endless cycle of mindless scrolling and constant notifications. Take Sarah, for example, who used to spend hours each day on social media, feeling drained and disconnected from the real world. Through digital minimalism, Sarah set boundaries around her screen time, leading to a newfound sense of focus and clarity in her daily life. As she reduced her reliance on technology, Sarah rediscovered her passion for painting and eventually turned it into a profitable side hustle. Her story illustrates how embracing a minimalist approach to digital consumption can open doors to new opportunities, creativity, and self-discovery. Ultimately, personal stories of transformation through digital minimalism serve as a testament to the profound impact this lifestyle change can have on one's well-being and overall happiness.

X. TOOLS AND TECHNIQUES FOR DIGITAL MINIMALISM

When implementing digital minimalism, it is crucial to explore various tools and techniques that can facilitate the process of disconnecting from excessive technology use. One effective tool is setting clear boundaries and creating designated tech-free zones in living or work spaces to promote mindfulness and focus. Additionally, utilizing time management techniques such as the Pomodoro method can help individuals break the cycle of constant digital distractions and improve productivity. Digital decluttering tools like apps that track screen time and block distracting websites can also be beneficial in reducing digital noise and promoting intentional technology use. Furthermore, practicing mindfulness and engaging in offline activities such as reading, exercising, or spending time in nature can help individuals cultivate a deeper sense of presence and fulfillment. By incorporating a combination of these tools and techniques, individuals can effectively navigate the digital landscape while fostering a healthier relationship with technology.

Software and apps that promote minimal digital usage

In today's digital age, the prevalence of software and apps that promote minimal digital usage is a testament to the growing awareness of the negative impact of excessive screen time on individuals' mental and physical well-being. These tools often provide features such as tracking screen time, setting limits on app usage, and encouraging mindfulness and intentional use of technology. By incorporating these software and apps into their daily routines, users can take control of their digital habits and cultivate a healthier relationship with technology. Rather than mindlessly scrolling through social media feeds or constantly checking notifications, individuals can now engage in more meaningful activities that promote creativity, focus, and human connection. As we strive for a more balanced approach to technology consumption, these digital minimalism tools serve as valuable resources in helping us disconnect from the digital noise and reconnect with the world around us.

Techniques for managing digital consumption

In the realm of digital consumption, there are several techniques that can be employed to manage the overwhelming influx of information and distractions that come with constant connectivity. One effective approach is prioritizing and setting boundaries on the use of technology. This may involve establishing specific time slots for checking email or social media, turning off notifications to minimize interruptions, or even opting for designated tech-free zones in your home or workplace. Additionally, incorporating mindfulness practices such as meditation or digital detox days can help to increase self-awareness and reduce reliance on digital devices. Creating a healthy balance between online and offline activities is crucial for mental well-being and productivity. By intentionally curating and controlling our digital habits, we can reclaim our time and focus on more meaningful pursuits in our lives. This conscious effort towards digital minimalism ultimately leads to a more fulfilling and balanced lifestyle.

Setting personal boundaries for digital use

In this digital age, setting personal boundaries for digital use is crucial for maintaining mental well-being and productivity. By establishing limits on screen time, social media consumption, and email checking, individuals can regain control over their time and attention. One effective strategy is to designate specific hours of the day for engaging with digital devices and creating technology-free zones in the home. This intentional approach to digital use allows for more meaningful interactions with others, increased focus on important tasks, and improved overall mental health. Furthermore, setting boundaries can also help individuals break free from the addictive nature of technology and cultivate a sense of autonomy over their digital habits. By taking proactive steps to create boundaries, individuals can experience the benefits of digital minimalism and achieve a better balance between their online and offline lives.

XI. CHALLENGES TO ADOPTING DIGITAL MINIMALISM

Adopting digital minimalism presents various challenges in to-day's technology-driven society. One significant obstacle is the fear of missing out (FOMO) that many individuals experience when considering reducing their digital usage. The constant stream of notifications, updates, and social media interactions makes it challenging to step back and detach from the digital world. Moreover, the pressure to constantly stay connected for work or social reasons can hinder efforts to embrace a more minimalist approach. Additionally, the addictive nature of tech-nology, reinforced by algorithms designed to keep users en-gaged, poses a major challenge to those attempting to limit their screen time. Overcoming these hurdles requires intentional effort, self-discipline, and a strong commitment to prioritizing real-life experiences over virtual ones. By recognizing and ad-dressing these challenges, individuals can gradually shift to-wards a more mindful and balanced relationship with technol-ogy.

Social pressures to remain digitally connected

The pervasive presence of social media and digital communica-tion platforms in today's society has created a sense of social pressure to remain digitally connected at all times. This pressure stems from the fear of missing out on important information, events, or social engagements. Individuals often feel the need to constantly check their devices and respond to messages promptly in order to stay in the loop and maintain social con-nections. The desire to be seen as active and engaged in the online world also contributes to this pressure, as individuals aim to present a curated version of themselves to their peers. Despite the benefits of staying connected, this constant digital engagement can lead to feelings of overwhelm, distraction, and even addiction. By understanding and acknowledging these social pressures, individuals can take steps towards practicing digital minimalism and learning to disconnect in order to prioritize their mental well-being and relationships.

Fear of missing out (FOMO)

The rise of digital technology has introduced a new phenomenon known as the Fear of Missing Out (FOMO), where individuals feel anxious and restless when they perceive that others are experiencing something exciting without them. This fear is exacerbated by the constant stream of updates and notifications from social media platforms, creating a sense of urgency to constantly check and stay connected. While FOMO may seem like a minor inconvenience, its implications on mental health and well-being should not be overlooked. The fear of missing out can lead to increased stress, anxiety, and feelings of inadequacy as individuals compare their lives to curated representations on social media. By embracing digital minimalism and consciously disconnecting from the constant barrage of information, individuals can regain control over their time and focus on meaningful experiences that bring genuine fulfillment. It is essential to recognize the impact of FOMO and take proactive steps towards cultivating a healthier relationship with technology for a more balanced and fulfilling life.

Overcoming initial withdrawal symptoms

As individuals embark on the journey of digital minimalism, they are likely to encounter initial withdrawal symptoms that can make the process challenging. These symptoms can range from feelings of anxiety and FOMO (fear of missing out) to a sense of restlessness and difficulty focusing. However, overcoming these initial hurdles is essential in order to reap the benefits of disconnecting from the digital world. By gradually reducing screen time, setting clear boundaries, and finding alternative activities to occupy one's time, individuals can successfully navigate through these withdrawal symptoms. It is important to recognize that these initial discomforts are often a sign of dependence on digital devices and that breaking free from this dependence is a necessary step towards achieving a healthier balance in life. Through perseverance and determination, individuals can overcome these obstacles and ultimately experience the positive impact of digital minimalism on their well-being and productivity.

XII. THE ROLE OF COMPANIES IN DIGITAL CONSUMPTION

As digital consumption continues to shape modern lifestyles, companies play a crucial role in influencing and driving this trend. From social media platforms to e-commerce giants, companies have the power to shape digital consumption patterns through targeted advertising, addictive design features, and personalized recommendations. By leveraging consumer data and algorithms, companies can create tailored experiences that encourage prolonged engagement with their products or services. This can lead to excessive screen time, decreased productivity, and even addiction to technology. However, companies also have the opportunity to promote digital minimalism by offering options for limiting notifications, setting usage limits, and promoting mindfulness in their design strategies. By acknowledging their impact on digital consumption habits and implementing measures to support a healthier balance, companies can contribute to a more mindful and intentional use of technology among consumers. Ultimately, the role of companies in digital consumption is pivotal in shaping the future of our digital landscape.

How companies encourage digital overuse

In today's digital age, companies utilize various tactics to encourage digital overuse among consumers. One common strategy is the design of addictive features within products and services, such as infinite scrolling, notifications, and personalized recommendations. These features are carefully engineered to keep users engaged for longer periods, thereby increasing the likelihood of overuse. Moreover, companies often employ persuasive marketing techniques to create a sense of FOMO (fear of missing out) and social pressure, pushing individuals to constantly check their devices for updates and notifications. Additionally, the gamification of digital platforms, with rewards systems and achievements, further incentivizes users to spend excessive amounts of time online. By understanding these tactics employed by companies, individuals can begin to reclaim control over their digital habits and strive towards a more balanced and mindful approach to technology usage.

Corporate responsibility in user digital health

Corporate responsibility in user digital health is a critical aspect that is often overlooked in the ongoing discussion of digital minimalism. As technology continues to shape our daily lives, companies must prioritize the well-being of their users by promoting healthy digital habits and providing transparent information about the impact of their products on mental and physical health. By implementing features that encourage mindfulness and limit screen time, corporations can play a key role in fostering a more balanced relationship with technology. Additionally, companies should invest in research to better understand the long-term effects of excessive digital use and work towards developing solutions that prioritize user well-being over profit margins. Ultimately, corporate responsibility in user digital health is a crucial component of the digital minimalism movement, highlighting the importance of ethical considerations in the design and promotion of technology.

Examples of ethical practices in technology firms

In examining ethical practices in technology firms, it is crucial to highlight examples of companies that prioritize transparency, data privacy, and social responsibility. For instance, Google's commitment to data protection can be seen in its implementation of privacy features such as two-factor authentication and robust encryption methods. Apple, on the other hand, is known for its dedication to ensuring the fair treatment of workers in its supply chain and reducing its environmental impact through renewable energy initiatives. Additionally, Salesforce's philanthropic efforts demonstrate a commitment to giving back to communities and supporting charitable causes. These examples showcase how technology firms can uphold ethical standards by safeguarding user data, promoting social welfare, and actively engaging in corporate social responsibility. By highlighting these practices, it becomes evident that ethical considerations are not just a trend but an integral part of operating in the tech industry.

XIII. LEGAL AND ETHICAL CONSIDERATIONS

As individuals strive to implement digital minimalism into their lives, it is essential to consider the legal and ethical implications of disconnecting from technology. On a legal front, issues concerning data privacy, intellectual property rights, and cybersecurity must be addressed. Users need to be aware of how their personal information is being collected, stored, and shared by online platforms, ensuring that they uphold their rights to privacy. Furthermore, respecting intellectual property rights and refraining from copyright infringement is crucial when engaging in digital activities. Ethically, it is important to consider the impact of digital consumption on mental health, social relationships, and overall well-being. Striking a balance between utilizing technology for productivity while also prioritizing human connection is paramount. By navigating these legal and ethical considerations, individuals can effectively navigate the digital landscape and cultivate a healthier relationship with technology.

Privacy concerns with digital minimalism tools

In the realm of digital minimalism, where individuals strive to reduce their reliance on technology to enhance their mental well-being, privacy concerns inevitably arise with the use of digital minimalism tools. While these tools can help individuals limit their screen time, declutter their digital lives, and prioritize real-world interactions, they also collect personal data that may compromise their privacy. Users must consider the trade-off between the benefits of these tools and the potential risks to their privacy. By using digital minimalism tools, individuals might inadvertently share sensitive information with third-party companies or hackers, leaving them vulnerable to data breaches or targeted advertisements. Therefore, it is essential for users to carefully read the privacy policies of these tools, understand how their data is being used, and take proactive steps to safeguard their privacy while engaging in digital minimalism practices. Ultimately, striking a balance between reaping the benefits of digital minimalism and protecting one's privacy is crucial in achieving a harmonious relationship with technology.

Ethical implications of data collection

As we delve deeper into the realm of digital minimalism, it becomes imperative to address the ethical implications of data collection. In today's digital age, personal information is constantly being harvested by various online platforms, often without our explicit consent. This raises concerns about privacy, consent, and the potential misuse of data for targeted advertising or even surveillance purposes. Moreover, the commodification of personal data has led to a culture of exploitation, where individuals are reduced to mere data points for profit. This raises serious questions about the ethical responsibility of tech companies, governments, and individuals in safeguarding the integrity and autonomy of personal information. As we strive to disconnect from the overwhelming digital noise, it is crucial to consider the ethical implications of data collection and advocate for greater transparency, accountability, and respect for privacy in the digital landscape. Only by addressing these ethical concerns can we truly achieve a balance between our digital lives and our well-being.

Legal frameworks supporting digital minimalism

One key aspect of digital minimalism is the legal frameworks that support its implementation. These frameworks play a crucial role in safeguarding individuals' rights to privacy, data protection, and freedom from online distractions. By enforcing regulations such as the General Data Protection Regulation (GDPR) in the European Union or the California Consumer Privacy Act (CCPA) in the United States, governments provide a level of control over how personal data is collected, stored, and used by online platforms. These laws empower individuals to make informed choices about their online presence and limit the intrusion of digital technologies into their daily lives. Additionally, legal frameworks can serve as a deterrent to tech companies that may prioritize profit over user well-being. In this way, the legal support for digital minimalism helps create a more balanced and mindful relationship with technology.

XIV. COMPARING DIGITAL MINIMALISM ACROSS CULTURES

In examining the concept of digital minimalism across different cultures, it becomes evident that the approach to disconnecting from technology varies significantly. While some societies place a high value on constant connectivity and digital presence, others prioritize offline interactions and traditional forms of communication. For example, Western cultures often struggle with the idea of digital minimalism due to the prevalence of social media and technology in daily life, leading to feelings of FOMO (fear of missing out) when attempting to disconnect. In contrast, Eastern cultures such as Japan have a more balanced relationship with technology, emphasizing the importance of mindfulness, solitude, and face-to-face connections. By comparing these cultural differences in attitudes towards digital minimalism, we can gain a deeper understanding of how societal norms and values shape individual behaviors and perceptions of technology use. Ultimately, exploring these variations can offer valuable insights into how different cultural contexts influence our relationship with digital devices and the benefits of embracing a more minimalist approach.

Digital minimalism in Eastern vs. Western societies

Western societies tend to embrace digital technology more rapidly and extensively than Eastern societies, leading to a stark contrast in approaches to digital minimalism. In Western cultures, the emphasis on individualism and consumerism often fuels a constant need for new gadgets and digital services, resulting in a culture of excess and overwhelm. On the other hand,

Eastern societies like Japan prioritize mindfulness, simplicity, and harmony, values that align well with the principles of digital minimalism. Japanese minimalism, for example, emphasizes quality over quantity and intentional engagement with technology rather than mindless consumption. This cultural difference underscores the varying attitudes towards digital minimalism, with Western societies seeing it as a means to unplug and detox from the digital world, while Eastern societies view it as a way to cultivate a more balanced and intentional relationship with technology. Ultimately, digital minimalism manifests differently in Eastern and Western societies, reflecting broader cultural values and norms.

Cultural attitudes towards technology use

Cultural attitudes towards technology use play a significant role in shaping how individuals interact with digital devices in their daily lives. In some societies, there is a strong emphasis on constantly being connected and always available online. This can lead to a culture of busyness and distraction, where individuals feel the need to constantly check their phones or respond to notifications. On the other hand, there are cultures that prioritize balance and moderation when it comes to technology use. These societies may value face-to-face interactions and quality time spent offline, fostering a healthier relationship with digital devices. By understanding the cultural attitudes towards technology use, individuals can reflect on their own habits and make adjustments to find a better balance that aligns with their values and priorities. Ultimately, being mindful of cultural influences can help individuals make more intentional choices about their technology use and lead to a more fulfilling and meaningful life.

Global movements and their local impacts

Global movements such as the rise of digital minimalism have significant impacts on local communities and individuals. The spread of this movement, advocating for a reduction in the use of digital technologies to reclaim focus and presence in daily life, has led to tangible changes in how people engage with technology at the local level. In cities and towns around the world, individuals are increasingly choosing to step back from the constant digital bombardment, seeking more meaningful connections in their immediate surroundings. This shift towards a more mindful use of technology has implications for local businesses, as consumers opt for experiences that prioritize real human interaction over virtual ones. Furthermore, the emphasis on digital detox and intentional technology use is fostering a sense of community as individuals come together to support each other in their journey towards a healthier digital lifestyle. Thus, global movements like digital minimalism are reshaping the way we interact with technology at the local level, promoting a more balanced and connected society.

XV. AGE AND DIGITAL MINIMALISM

As individuals age, their relationship with technology and digital devices often evolves. Younger generations may be more inclined to embrace the constant connectivity and stimuli offered by the digital world, while older individuals might seek a more simplified and mindful approach. Digital minimalism, with its emphasis on intentional technology use and deliberate disconnection, can be particularly beneficial for older adults looking to strike a balance between staying connected and avoiding information overload. By adopting a minimalist approach to technology, older individuals can focus on what truly matters to them, whether it be meaningful interactions with loved ones or pursuing personal interests without the distraction of constant notifications. Embracing digital minimalism in later stages of life can lead to increased clarity, reduced stress, and a newfound sense of control over one's digital habits.

Adoption of digital minimalism among different age groups

The adoption of digital minimalism varies among different age groups, reflecting the distinct ways individuals interact with technology based on their generational experiences. Younger generations, such as Gen Z and Millennials, tend to be early adopters of digital minimalism due to growing concerns about the negative impacts of excessive screen time on mental health and productivity. They are more likely to embrace minimalist practices like setting strict boundaries on device usage and prioritizing face-to-face interactions. In contrast, older age groups, like Baby Boomers and Gen X, may be slower to adopt digital minimalism, as they have been accustomed to the pervasive presence of technology in their lives. However, as awareness of the benefits of disconnecting and reducing digital clutter spreads, more individuals across all age groups are beginning to incorporate elements of digital minimalism into their daily routines for a healthier and more balanced lifestyle.

Tailoring digital minimalism strategies for the elderly

When tailoring digital minimalism strategies for the elderly, it is important to take into consideration their unique needs and challenges. Many older adults may not be as familiar with technology as younger generations, so a patient and personalized approach is key. One effective strategy is to focus on simplifying their devices and minimizing distractions. This can involve decluttering their home screens, limiting notifications, and teaching them how to use only the essential functions of their devices. Additionally, providing clear and step-by-step instructions can help them feel more comfortable navigating the digital world. Encouraging regular breaks from screens and promoting offline activities can also benefit their overall well-being. By adapting digital minimalism techniques to suit the needs of the elderly, we can help them better manage their digital usage and enjoy a more balanced and fulfilling life in today's tech-driven world.

Digital education for younger generations

In the digital age, incorporating technology into education for younger generations has become increasingly prevalent. Digital education offers a wide range of benefits, such as enhanced engagement, interactive learning opportunities, and access to a wealth of information. By utilizing digital tools, educators can cater to different learning styles and provide personalized learning experiences for students. Additionally, digital education can help bridge the gap between traditional classroom learning and real-world applications, preparing students for the ever-evolving job market. However, it is crucial to find a balance and ensure that digital education does not overshadow the importance of critical thinking, creativity, and interpersonal skills. By embracing digital education while also emphasizing the value of disconnecting and cultivating these essential skills, younger generations can be better equipped to thrive in the digital age.

XVI. GENDER PERSPECTIVES ON DIGITAL MINIMALISM

A gender perspective on digital minimalism unveils unique considerations and challenges that women and men may face in adopting a minimalist approach to technology. In a society where traditional gender roles and expectations still linger, women often find themselves juggling multiple responsibilities, both at work and home. For women, digital minimalism may offer a respite from the constant demands of technology, allowing them to reclaim their time and mental energy. On the other hand, men may encounter different pressures in their professional and personal lives, leading to a different set of digital habits and dependencies. Understanding how gender norms intersect with digital minimalism can shed light on the diverse ways in which individuals navigate their relationship with technology. By acknowledging these gender-specific perspectives, we can tailor our approach to digital minimalism to address the unique needs and challenges faced by different genders.

How men and women differently approach digital minimalism

Men and women often approach digital minimalism in different ways due to societal expectations and individual preferences. Men may be more inclined to adopt a minimalist lifestyle in order to increase productivity and efficiency, viewing technology as a tool to streamline tasks and improve overall performance. On the other hand, women may see digital minimalism as a way to create space for mindfulness and self-care, focusing on reducing digital clutter to prioritize mental well-being and personal growth. These gendered perspectives can influence how individuals choose to disconnect from technology, with men leaning towards strict boundaries and rules, while women may opt for a more intuitive and flexible approach. Regardless of gender, the key to successful digital minimalism lies in finding a balance that aligns with one's values and goals, allowing for a healthier relationship with technology and a more fulfilling life overall.

Gender-specific challenges in digital minimalism

Gender-specific challenges in digital minimalism can present unique obstacles for individuals. Women, in particular, may face pressures to maintain an online presence that aligns with societal expectations of femininity, leading to increased time spent on social media and digital platforms. This can result in a heightened sense of comparison and self-doubt, as women navigate the curated images and lifestyles presented by others online. Conversely, men may struggle with the pressure to be constantly connected and available in the digital realm, impacting their ability to disconnect and prioritize real-world relationships. Additionally, gender norms around technology use can influence how individuals approach digital minimalism, with women often encouraged to engage in self-care practices that involve technology, while men may be more focused on productivity and efficiency. Understanding these gender-specific challenges is crucial in developing strategies for achieving a healthier balance with technology in today's digital age.

Case studies of gender-focused digital minimalism initiatives

In exploring case studies of gender-focused digital minimalism initiatives, it becomes evident that gender plays a significant role in shaping individuals' relationships with technology. Women, in particular, have been found to experience higher levels of digital burnout and overwhelm due to societal expectations and gender norms that often result in a disproportionate burden of multitasking and caregiving responsibilities. As a result, initiatives aimed at promoting digital minimalism among women have emerged, highlighting the importance of creating spaces for self-care, mindfulness, and disconnecting from technology. These initiatives not only address the unique challenges faced by women in the digital age but also emphasize the need for a more inclusive approach to digital wellness that takes into account diverse gender identities and experiences. By examining these case studies, we can gain valuable insights into how digital minimalism can be tailored to address the specific needs and concerns of different gender groups, ultimately leading to a more balanced and fulfilling life for all.

XVII. ECONOMIC IMPACTS OF DIGITAL MINIMALISM

When considering the economic impacts of digital minimalism, it becomes apparent that this lifestyle choice can have significant effects on various industries and sectors. By reducing the time spent on digital devices and social media platforms, individuals may find themselves less tempted by online shopping, leading to a decrease in impulsive purchases and a shift towards more intentional and mindful consumption habits. This change in consumer behavior could potentially disrupt traditional marketing strategies and require businesses to adapt their approaches to reach their target audience effectively. Additionally, the rise of digital minimalism may result in a decline in digital advertising revenue for tech giants, prompting them to reevaluate their business models and consider alternative sources of income. Overall, the economic landscape stands to be reshaped by the growing popularity of digital minimalism as individuals prioritize real-world experiences over constant connectivity.

Cost savings associated with reduced digital consumption

Digital minimalism not only contributes to a more fulfilling life but also presents financial benefits through reduced digital consumption. By curating our online activities and focusing only on essential digital tools or platforms, we can significantly decrease the amount of time spent online. This decrease in screen time translates to lower utility bills, reduced data usage, and potential savings on subscription services. In today's digital age, where streaming services, apps, and online purchases can easily add up, practicing digital minimalism can lead to tangible cost savings. Furthermore, the shift towards more intentional technology use can also help individuals avoid impulse buying or subscriptions, ultimately contributing to a more mindful and economical approach to their digital lifestyle. In essence, by prioritizing quality over quantity, individuals not only save money but also gain a sense of control and satisfaction over their digital habits.

Economic benefits for individuals and businesses

Digital minimalism offers significant economic benefits for individuals and businesses.

By cutting down on excessive screen time and digital distractions, individuals can reclaim valuable time that can be redirected towards more productive activities, such as focusing on personal growth, pursuing hobbies, or engaging in face-to-face interactions. This increased productivity can lead to improved job performance, ultimately equating to potential career advancements and higher earning potential. For businesses, encouraging digital minimalism can result in enhanced employee efficiency and creativity, as well as reduced operational costs related to unnecessary technology usage. Moreover, businesses can benefit from a more engaged and present workforce, leading to increased collaboration and innovation within the organization. Overall, implementing digital minimalism practices can not only bring positive economic outcomes for individuals but also for businesses looking to optimize their resources and workforce.

Long-term economic predictions related to digital minimalism trends

As digital minimalism continues to gain traction in our society, it is crucial to consider the long-term economic implications of this trend. By reducing our reliance on technology and social media, individuals may spend less money on unnecessary gadgets, apps, and subscriptions, leading to a decrease in consumerism and materialism. This shift towards a more intentional and mindful approach to technology consumption could potentially disrupt industries that thrive on constant digital engagement, such as advertising and online retail. However, this movement may also create opportunities for businesses that prioritize quality over quantity and focus on providing value to their customers. As more people embrace digital minimalism, we may see a shift towards a more sustainable and ethical economy, where people prioritize meaningful experiences over material possessions, fostering a more balanced and fulfilling way of life.

XVIII. ENVIRONMENTAL CONSIDERATIONS

In the context of digital minimalism, environmental considerations play a crucial role in shaping our technological habits and overall well-being. The increasing reliance on electronic devices contributes to a significant environmental footprint, from the production and disposal of these devices to the energy consumption required to power them. As individuals strive to disconnect and lead more intentional digital lives, it is essential to consider the environmental impact of our tech consumption. By reducing our dependence on technology through digital minimalism, we can lessen our contribution to electronic waste and lower our energy consumption, ultimately leading to a more sustainable lifestyle. By being mindful of the environmental consequences of our digital choices, we can work towards a healthier balance between technology and the natural world, fostering a more harmonious relationship between our digital lives and the environment.

Reduction in electronic waste through minimalism

Embracing minimalism in the digital realm can significantly reduce electronic waste. By adopting a minimalist approach to technology, individuals can prioritize quality over quantity, leading to fewer gadgets being purchased and discarded. This conscious decision to own only what is truly necessary not only minimizes the demand for new electronics but also encourages the longevity of devices through proper care and maintenance. Additionally, digital minimalism promotes the practice of repairing or refurbishing electronics instead of automatically discarding them when they encounter minor issues. By extending the lifespan of electronic devices, the overall environmental impact of manufacturing, transportation, and disposal can be significantly reduced. Ultimately, incorporating minimalist principles into our digital consumption habits can contribute to a more sustainable future by lessening the environmental burden of electronic waste.

Energy savings and sustainability benefits

One of the significant benefits of practicing digital minimalism is the potential for energy savings and increased sustainability. By reducing our dependency on digital devices and the internet, we can decrease our energy consumption, particularly in terms of electricity usage. From limiting screen time to powering down electronic devices when not in use, every effort towards digital minimalism contributes to a smaller carbon footprint. Additionally, digital minimalism encourages a more mindful approach to consumption, which can lead to less electronic waste being generated. Over time, adopting a minimalist mindset towards technology can result in a more sustainable lifestyle that is beneficial not only for the individual but also for the environment as a whole. By consciously choosing quality over quantity and focusing on what truly adds value to our lives, we can contribute to a more eco-friendly future while reaping the personal rewards of a less cluttered digital existence.

Promoting environmental consciousness through digital minimalism

In a world inundated with digital distractions, promoting environmental consciousness through digital minimalism can serve as a powerful tool in fostering a more sustainable relationship with technology. By intentionally reducing screen time and streamlining digital activities, individuals can minimize their carbon footprint by consuming less energy and reducing electronic waste. Embracing a minimalist approach to technology not only benefits the environment but also encourages mindfulness and intentionality in daily life. By disconnecting from the constant barrage of notifications and notifications, individuals can re-focus their attention on the natural world around them, leading to a deeper appreciation for the environment and a sense of stewardship towards the planet. Ultimately, by promoting environmental consciousness through digital minimalism, individuals can play a crucial role in mitigating the impact of technology on the environment while cultivating a more balanced and mindful way of living.

XIX. FUTURE OF DIGITAL MINIMALISM

As society continues to grapple with the implications of a hyperconnected world, the future of digital minimalism appears both promising and challenging. With the increasing availability of technology in every aspect of our lives, the need to disconnect and regain control over our digital habits is more pressing than ever. Moving forward, the conversation around digital minimalism is likely to shift towards advocating for intentional and mindful use of technology rather than complete avoidance. This adaptive approach recognizes the importance of technology in modern life while emphasizing the need for boundaries and self-regulation. By promoting a balanced relationship with technology, digital minimalism can help individuals harness the benefits of digital tools without succumbing to their addictive nature. As we navigate the evolving landscape of digital culture, embracing the principles of digital minimalism offers a roadmap for a healthier and more fulfilling relationship with technology.

Emerging trends in digital minimalism

In today's fast-paced society, emerging trends in digital minimalism are becoming increasingly popular as individuals seek to disconnect from the constant stimulation of technology and focus on living a more intentional and present life. This trend encourages individuals to evaluate their relationship with digital devices and consider how they can minimize their screen time to create a healthier balance. By adopting digital minimalism practices, individuals can experience increased mindfulness, improved mental health, and enhanced productivity. Through limiting the use of social media, reducing digital clutter, and setting boundaries with technology, individuals can regain control over their time and attention, allowing them to prioritize activities that bring them joy and fulfillment. Embracing the principles of digital minimalism can help individuals cultivate a sense of purpose and connection in a world that is increasingly driven by constant connectivity and technological distractions.

Predictions for digital minimalism's growth

As society becomes more aware of the negative impacts of constant digital connectivity, the growth of digital minimalism is predicted to accelerate in the coming years. As individuals seek ways to reclaim their time, focus, and mental well-being, the principles of digital minimalism offer a compelling solution. By intentionally reducing screen time, limiting social media use, and curating digital tools to enhance rather than detract from life, people are able to cultivate deeper relationships, pursue meaningful hobbies, and prioritize self-care. As this shift towards a more mindful and intentional approach to technology continues to gain momentum, we can expect to see an increase in the popularity of digital detox retreats, minimalist phone apps, and community support networks for those looking to disconnect in a hyper-connected world. Ultimately, the growing interest in digital minimalism signifies a broader cultural desire for balance, presence, and authentic human connection in an increasingly digitized world.

Potential new areas for applying digital minimalism principles

When considering potential new areas for applying digital minimalism principles, it is important to look beyond the individual and into larger societal contexts. One area that could benefit from implementing these principles is education. As technology continues to play a significant role in the classroom, students are often bombarded with distractions that hinder their ability to focus and learn efficiently. By incorporating digital minimalism practices in the educational setting, such as limiting screen time and promoting more meaningful online interactions, students may experience improved academic performance and better retention of information. Additionally, the workplace is another area ripe for the application of digital minimalism. With the rise of remote work and the constant barrage of emails and notifications, employees can easily become overwhelmed and stressed. By encouraging digital detoxes, setting boundaries around technology use, and fostering a culture of mindful communication, organizations can create a more productive and balanced work environment. Ultimately, exploring new avenues for applying digital minimalism principles can lead to positive outcomes not only on an individual level but also on a broader societal scale.

XX. ROLE OF EDUCATION IN PROMOTING DIGITAL MINIMALISM

In the realm of digital minimalism, education plays a crucial role in promoting a healthier relationship with technology. By teaching individuals about the importance of intentional and mindful use of digital devices, educators can empower students to cultivate self-discipline and prioritize real-world interactions over screen time. Through educational initiatives, students can learn to set boundaries, limit their consumption of digital content, and embrace activities that foster creativity, critical thinking, and social connections. Furthermore, education can instill in individuals the awareness of the potential negative impacts of excessive screen time on mental health, productivity, and overall well-being. By equipping students with the knowledge and tools to practice digital minimalism, educational institutions can help shape a generation that values balance, focus, and authentic human connections in the digital age.

Curriculum development for digital minimalism

In adapting curriculum development for digital minimalism, educators must prioritize teaching students the skills necessary to navigate the digital world with intentionality and mindfulness. This includes emphasizing critical thinking and discernment when engaging with technology, as well as promoting healthy boundaries and self-regulation in their usage. Incorporating lessons on digital detoxing and the importance of unplugging periodically can help students develop a balanced relationship with technology, rather than being consumed by it. Additionally, offering courses on digital literacy and cyber hygiene can empower students to make informed choices about their online presence and protect their digital well-being. By integrating these principles into the curriculum, educators can equip students with the tools needed to thrive in a technology-driven society while maintaining a healthy balance between their online and offline lives.

Educator roles in fostering minimal digital usage

To foster minimal digital usage, educators play a crucial role in guiding students towards healthy technology habits. One way educators can achieve this is by modeling balanced digital behavior themselves. By setting limits on their own digital usage and establishing boundaries, teachers can demonstrate the importance of disconnecting and being present in the moment. Additionally, educators can incorporate lessons on digital wellness into their curriculum, teaching students about the benefits of limiting screen time and the potential negative effects of excessive digital consumption. Encouraging activities that promote face-to-face interactions and offline engagement can also help students develop a healthier relationship with technology. By actively promoting minimal digital usage and emphasizing the importance of disconnecting, educators can empower students to prioritize their well-being and mental health over constant digital distractions.

Student-led initiatives promoting minimalism

Student-led initiatives promoting minimalism can play a significant role in fostering a culture of mindfulness and intentionality among university communities. By organizing events, work-shops, and campaigns that highlight the importance of reducing clutter and distractions in both physical and digital spaces, students can inspire their peers to embrace a simpler, more focused lifestyle. These initiatives can provide practical tips and strategies for decluttering physical spaces, managing digital devices more effectively, and prioritizing meaningful interactions over constant connectivity. Additionally, student-led minimalism movements can create a sense of community and support for those looking to make positive changes in their lives. By encouraging mindfulness and intentionality in all aspects of daily routines, these initiatives can empower students to lead more balanced and fulfilling lives both on and off campus. Ultimately, student-led efforts to promote minimalism can contribute to a healthier and more sustainable college experience for all.

XXI. DIGITAL MINIMALISM AND LEISURE ACTIVITIES

In the realm of leisure activities, digital minimalism offers a refreshing approach to reclaiming quality time for meaningful experiences. By intentionally reducing screen time and app usage, individuals can rediscover the joys of traditional hobbies like reading, gardening, or painting. Engaging in these analog pursuits can offer a sense of fulfillment and relaxation that is often overshadowed by the constant distractions of the digital world. Moreover, by disconnecting from the online sphere, individuals can cultivate deeper connections with themselves and those around them. This intentional shift towards minimalism in leisure activities encourages a more mindful approach to how free time is spent, fostering a genuine sense of presence and contentment. Ultimately, embracing digital minimalism in leisure activities can lead to a more balanced and fulfilling life.

Rediscovering offline hobbies and interests

In today's digital age, many individuals find themselves constantly glued to screens, whether it be for work, social media, or entertainment. However, amidst this digital saturation, there is a growing movement towards rediscovering offline hobbies and interests. Engaging in activities such as painting, gardening, reading, or baking can provide a much-needed break from the constant stimulation of technology. These offline pursuits not only offer a reprieve from screen time but also have been shown to improve mental well-being and creativity. By disconnecting from the digital world and immersing oneself in the tangible and sensory experiences of offline hobbies, individuals can cultivate a deeper sense of fulfillment and satisfaction in their lives. In a society where technology dominates so much of our time and attention, rediscovering offline hobbies and interests can serve as a way to reconnect with ourselves and find a more balanced and meaningful existence.

Impact on sports and outdoor activities

One significant impact of digital minimalism on society is its effect on sports and outdoor activities. With the rise of smartphones and social media, individuals are becoming increasingly glued to their screens, leading to a decrease in physical activity and time spent outdoors. This can have detrimental effects on both physical and mental health, as exercise and fresh air are essential for overall well-being. Moreover, the constant distraction of technology can detract from the immersive experience of engaging in sports or outdoor activities, hindering one's ability to fully enjoy the present moment. By practicing digital minimalism, individuals can reclaim their time and focus, allowing them to prioritize physical activity and outdoor pursuits. This shift can lead to a more balanced and fulfilling lifestyle, promoting better overall health and enriching experiences in nature.

Revival of traditional forms of entertainment

In today's fast-paced digital world, there has been a noticeable revival of traditional forms of entertainment. As people become more aware of the negative impact of constant screen time on their mental and physical well-being, they are seeking out alternative ways to relax and unwind. This resurgence can be seen in the popularity of activities like board games, live theater, and outdoor concerts. By engaging in these traditional forms of entertainment, individuals are able to disconnect from their devices and truly be present in the moment. These activities also foster a sense of community and connection, as they often involve face-to-face interaction with others. In a society that is increasingly dominated by technology, the revival of traditional entertainment is a refreshing reminder of the simple pleasures that can be found offline. By embracing these age-old pastimes, individuals can strike a healthier balance between their digital and analog lives.

XXII. HEALTH AND WELLNESS MOVEMENTS RELATED TO DIGITAL MINIMALISM

In the context of health and wellness movements, digital minimalism has emerged as a powerful tool for individuals seeking to reclaim control over their screen time and find balance in their lives. By prioritizing intentional technology use and limiting the constant influx of notifications and distractions, adherents of digital minimalism are able to focus more on their physical and mental well-being. This movement encourages people to be more present in the moment, engage in meaningful face-to-face interactions, and prioritize activities that promote overall health. Through embracing digital minimalism, individuals can reduce stress, improve sleep quality, and foster a greater sense of mindfulness in their daily routines. By disconnecting from the constant barrage of digital stimuli, individuals can reconnect with themselves, their surroundings, and ultimately enhance their overall quality of life. The shift towards digital minimalism in the realm of health and wellness underscores the importance of finding a harmonious balance between technology and personal well-being.

Integration with physical wellness programs

With the rise of digital technology and its pervasive presence in our lives, there has been a growing concern about the negative impact it can have on our physical well-being. One way to address this issue is through integration with physical wellness programs. By incorporating digital minimalism practices into fitness routines or health programs, individuals can create a more balanced approach to their overall well-being. For example, using technology to track exercise progress can be beneficial, but setting boundaries to prevent over-reliance on devices is crucial. Additionally, incorporating mindfulness practices into digital detox sessions can help individuals become more aware of their physical and mental state, leading to a more holistic approach to wellness. By integrating digital minimalism with physical wellness programs, individuals can cultivate a healthier relationship with technology while prioritizing their physical health.

Mental health initiatives incorporating minimalism

In the realm of mental health initiatives, the concept of minimalism has gained traction for its ability to promote emotional well-being and reduce stress levels. By encouraging individuals to declutter their physical spaces and streamline their possessions, minimalism can also have a positive impact on mental clarity and focus. In the context of digital minimalism, this approach extends to the realm of technology and online consumption. Embracing digital minimalism involves deliberate decision-making about the apps, websites, and devices we engage with, prioritizing quality over quantity. By setting boundaries for screen time, limiting distractions, and curating a more intentional digital experience, individuals can create a healthier relationship with technology and improve their overall mental health. In a world saturated with constant stimulation, practicing digital minimalism offers a valuable opportunity for self-care and self-preservation in the digital age.

Wellness retreats focusing on digital detoxification

Wellness retreats focusing on digital detoxification have become increasingly popular in response to the constant presence of technology in our lives. These retreats offer individuals the opportunity to disconnect from their devices and reconnect with themselves and nature. By taking a break from screens and notifications, participants can experience improved mental clarity, reduced stress levels, and better sleep quality. The structured programs at these retreats often include mindfulness practices, outdoor activities, and holistic treatments to promote overall well-being. Additionally, digital detox retreats provide a space for reflection and self-discovery, allowing individuals to reassess their relationship with technology and establish healthier boundaries moving forward. As our society becomes increasingly dependent on digital devices, these retreats offer a much-needed reprieve and a chance to prioritize self-care and mental health in a technology-driven world.

XXIII. DIGITAL MINIMALISM IN DEVELOPING COUNTRIES

As developing countries navigate the complexities of digitalization, the concept of digital minimalism can provide valuable insights into managing the impacts of technology on societies with limited resources. In these regions, where access to technology may be unevenly distributed, practicing digital minimalism can help individuals and communities make deliberate choices about how they engage with digital tools. By focusing on essential uses of technology and reducing distractions, developing countries can optimize the benefits of digital tools while minimizing potential negative effects such as information overload and social isolation. Embracing digital minimalism in these contexts can empower individuals to prioritize meaningful interactions and activities, fostering a more balanced relationship with technology that aligns with the needs and values of their communities. In doing so, developing countries can harness the power of digital tools for positive social and economic development while safeguarding against the risks of unchecked digital consumption.

Unique challenges and opportunities

Digital minimalism presents both unique challenges and opportunities for individuals seeking a healthier relationship with technology. On one hand, embracing a minimalist approach to digital consumption can be daunting, especially in a society that values constant connectivity. The pressure to be constantly available and engaged online can make it difficult to detach from screens and prioritize real-world interactions. However, by reducing digital distractions, individuals have the opportunity to reclaim their time and attention for more meaningful pursuits. This shift can lead to increased focus, productivity, and overall well-being. Embracing digital minimalism also opens the door to exploring new hobbies, connecting with nature, and fostering deep, offline relationships. By navigating the challenges and seizing the opportunities presented by digital minimalism, individuals can cultivate a more balanced and fulfilling life.

Case studies from various developing nations

When examining case studies from various developing nations, we can observe the impact of digital minimalism on individuals and communities. In countries where technological access is still limited, practicing digital minimalism can lead to increased focus, productivity, and overall well-being. For example, in rural areas of India where internet connectivity is sparse, individuals who intentionally limit their screen time have reported higher levels of satisfaction and fulfillment in their daily lives. Similarly, in parts of Africa where smartphones are not as ubiquitous, those who prioritize real-world interactions over digital distractions have shown greater resilience to mental health issues. These case studies highlight the transformative power of disconnecting from technology and embracing a more intentional approach to digital consumption in developing nations. By learning from these examples, individuals worldwide can adopt digital minimalism as a tool for personal growth and societal progress.

Strategies tailored for lower-tech environments

In lower-tech environments, strategies for disconnecting and embracing digital minimalism may need to be adapted to suit the available resources. One approach could be to focus on creating physical barriers to technology use, such as designating specific areas in the home or workplace as tech-free zones. This can help individuals better separate their digital and real-world activities, fostering a healthier balance. Additionally, promoting alternatives to technology, such as outdoor activities, hobbies, or reading physical books, can help individuals reduce their reliance on digital devices. Encouraging mindfulness and awareness of digital consumption can also be beneficial in lower-tech environments, as individuals may be more likely to use technology intentionally rather than out of habit. By tailoring strategies to the specific challenges and opportunities presented by lower-tech environments, individuals can successfully disconnect and lead a more fulfilling and balanced life.

XXIV. RESISTANCE AND CRITICISM OF DIGITAL MINIMALISM

Criticism of digital minimalism stems from various perspectives, with some arguing that it promotes a sense of disconnection and isolation. Critics believe that by reducing our reliance on digital tools and platforms, we risk losing touch with the interconnected world around us. They view digital minimalism as a retreat from the modern way of life, emphasizing the importance of staying plugged in to remain informed and connected. However, proponents of digital minimalism argue that it is precisely this constant connectivity that leads to feelings of overwhelm, distraction, and anxiety. By intentionally limiting our digital consumption, we can reclaim our time, focus, and mental clarity. Rather than isolating ourselves, digital minimalism encourages a more mindful and intentional approach to tech use, fostering deeper connections with others and ourselves. Ultimately, the resistance and criticism of digital minimalism highlight the ongoing debate surrounding the role of technology in our lives and the power of intentional disconnection.

Critiques from technology advocates

Technology advocates have not unanimously embraced the principles of digital minimalism. While some acknowledge the benefits of disconnecting from the constant barrage of digital distractions, others argue that technology is an essential tool for communication, productivity, and innovation. These advocates contend that rather than disengaging from technology, individuals should learn how to use it mindfully and purposefully. They believe that by leveraging the advantages of technology, individuals can enhance their personal and professional lives in meaningful ways. However, critics of this perspective argue that the pervasive nature of technology in today's society has led to a loss of focus, increased stress, and a decrease in real-life social connections. They suggest that by adopting the principles of digital minimalism, individuals can regain control over their attention and reclaim their autonomy from the grip of technology. Ultimately, the debate between technology advocates highlights the complex relationship between humans and technology in the digital age.

Challenges in measuring the impact of digital minimalism

One of the key challenges in measuring the impact of digital minimalism is the subjective nature of its benefits. While traditional metrics like screen time or social media usage can provide some quantitative data, they fail to capture the qualitative changes that digital minimalism can bring about. For instance, improved mental well-being, increased focus, and enhanced productivity are outcomes that are harder to quantify with numbers alone. Additionally, the long-term effects of digital minimalism may not be immediately apparent, making it challenging to assess its true impact over time. Moreover, individual differences in how people engage with technology and the varying definitions of what constitutes digital minimalism further complicate measurement efforts. To accurately evaluate the impact of digital minimalism, a more holistic approach that considers both quantitative and qualitative aspects is needed, alongside longitudinal studies to track changes in behavior and well-being over an extended period.

Addressing misconceptions about digital minimalism

In today's fast-paced digital world, there exists a common misconception that digital minimalism means completely cutting oneself off from technology. However, this is not the case. Digital minimalism is not about abandoning technology altogether, but rather about using it more intentionally and mindfully. It is about consciously choosing the digital tools and platforms that add value to your life, while eliminating or reducing those that do not. By addressing this misconception, individuals can see that digital minimalism is a practical and sustainable approach to reclaiming their time and attention in a world filled with distractions. It offers a way to strike a healthy balance between the benefits of technology and the need for mental clarity and focused productivity. By understanding the true essence of digital minimalism, individuals can embark on a transformative journey towards a more mindful and fulfilling existence.

XXV. PERSONALIZATION OF DIGITAL MINIMALISM

In the realm of digital minimalism, the personalization of one's approach is crucial for its effectiveness. XXV. Personalization of Digital Minimalism emphasizes the need for individuals to tailor their strategies to their unique habits, preferences, and life-styles. By recognizing that not all techniques will work universally, this chapter advocates for a personalized approach that allows individuals to disconnect from technology in a way that is most meaningful and sustainable for them. Whether it involves setting specific boundaries on social media usage, de-cluttering digital spaces, or implementing regular tech-free periods, customization is key to successfully incorporating digital minimalism into one's life. This chapter underscores the importance of self-awareness and experimentation in finding the balance that works best for each individual, ultimately leading to a more intentional and fulfilling relationship with technology.

Customizing minimalism to fit individual needs

In the quest for achieving digital minimalism, it is essential to recognize that the concept is not a one-size-fits-all solution. Each individual's needs, preferences, and circumstances are unique, requiring a personalized approach to minimalism. Customizing minimalism to fit individual needs involves a thoughtful assessment of one's digital habits and a willingness to make targeted changes that align with personal goals. By tailoring minimalism to suit specific requirements, individuals can better address their challenges and optimize their digital well-being.

This customization may involve setting boundaries with technology, choosing specific apps or tools that best serve their purposes, or establishing regular digital detox routines that work for them. Ultimately, the key to successful digital minimalism lies in adapting the principles of simplicity and intentionality to one's own lifestyle, allowing for a more meaningful and fulfilling relationship with technology.

Personal success stories

One personal success story that exemplifies the benefits of digital minimalism is that of Sarah, a busy professional in her mid-thirties. Faced with mounting stress and burnout from constantly being plugged in, Sarah decided to take a step back and reassess her relationship with technology. She began by setting clear boundaries for herself, like limiting social media usage and turning off notifications on her phone. As a result, Sarah found herself feeling more present in her daily interactions, more focused at work, and less overwhelmed by the constant barrage of information. By decluttering her digital life, Sarah was able to reclaim her time and energy, leading to increased productivity and overall satisfaction. Her success story serves as a testament to the transformative power of embracing a minimalist approach to technology for achieving a healthier work-life balance.

Guides for creating personal digital minimalism plans

One key aspect of creating a personal digital minimalism plan is to start by identifying your priorities and values. This step involves reflecting on what truly matters to you in terms of relationships, work, hobbies, and personal growth. By understanding your core values, you can then align your digital usage with those values, ensuring that your time online is spent purposefully and intentionally. Following this self-assessment, it is important to set clear boundaries and limits for your digital interactions. This may include designating specific times for checking emails or social media, limiting screen time before bed, or establishing technology-free zones in your home. By creating these boundaries, you can regain control over your digital habits and prevent mindless scrolling or constant connectivity. Ultimately, developing a personal digital minimalism plan requires a deep understanding of your values and boundaries, which can then guide your digital choices to create a more balanced and fulfilling life.

XXVI. DIGITAL MINIMALISM AND CONSUMER BEHAVIOR

In today's digital age, consumer behavior is heavily influenced by the prevalence of technology in our daily lives. Digital minimalism, a philosophy that advocates for limiting one's digital distractions to focus on what truly matters, has the potential to reshape consumer behavior patterns. By consciously disconnecting from the constant barrage of notifications and online stimuli, individuals can regain control over their purchasing decisions. When we are not constantly bombarded with targeted ads and social media influencers promoting products, we become more mindful of our spending habits and are less susceptible to impulse buys. This shift towards digital minimalism encourages individuals to prioritize experiences over material possessions, leading to a more intentional and fulfilling lifestyle. As consumers become more mindful of their digital consumption, they can make more informed choices that align with their values and goals, ultimately leading to a more satisfying and balanced life.

Changes in purchasing patterns

In today's fast-paced digital world, changes in purchasing patterns have become increasingly evident as technology continues to evolve. With the rise of e-commerce platforms and the convenience of online shopping, consumers are now more inclined to make purchases with just a few clicks of a button. This shift towards digital transactions has not only transformed the way people shop but has also influenced the way businesses market their products and services. Companies now have to adapt to these changing consumer behaviors by optimizing their online presence and providing a seamless shopping experience. Additionally, the accessibility of information on the internet has empowered consumers to make more informed purchasing decisions, leading to a greater emphasis on quality and value. As the landscape of retail continues to evolve, understanding these changes in purchasing patterns is essential for businesses to stay competitive and relevant in the digital age.

Impact on advertising and marketing

Digital minimalism has had a profound impact on the world of advertising and marketing. With more individuals opting for a simplified and intentional approach to their digital consumption, traditional advertising strategies are being challenged. Marketers are now faced with the task of creating more meaningful and authentic content that resonates with their audience on a deeper level. Rather than bombarding consumers with endless ads and promotions, companies are now focusing on building genuine relationships and providing value to their customers. This shift towards quality over quantity has forced advertisers to think outside the box and come up with innovative ways to engage with their target demographic. By embracing digital minimalism, businesses can establish trust and loyalty among consumers, leading to long-term success in a cluttered online marketplace. This new era of marketing requires creativity, empathy, and a keen understanding of human behavior in the digital age.

Consumer awareness and education about digital products

Consumer awareness and education about digital products play a crucial role in promoting responsible and mindful use of technology. By understanding the potential risks and benefits associated with digital consumption, individuals can make more informed decisions about the products they choose to engage with. This awareness can empower consumers to protect their personal data, safeguard their privacy, and navigate the digital landscape more effectively. Furthermore, education about digital products can help users develop critical thinking skills to discern between credible information and misinformation online. In an era where digital technologies are ubiquitous, fostering consumer awareness and education is essential for promoting digital literacy and fostering a more balanced and intentional relationship with technology. Ultimately, by prioritizing consumer awareness and education, individuals can harness the benefits of digital products while minimizing the potential drawbacks and pitfalls that come with excessive digital consumption.

XXVII. DIGITAL MINIMALISM AND PUBLIC POLICY

One of the key implications of digital minimalism for public policy lies in the realm of privacy and data protection. As individuals become more intentional about the digital technologies they engage with, there is growing awareness of the need for stronger regulations to safeguard personal information. Public policymakers must address concerns related to data breaches, surveillance, and the ethical use of consumer data by corporations. By promoting digital minimalism, governments can encourage a more conscious approach to technology use that prioritizes individual autonomy and privacy. Additionally, digital minimalism can have broader societal benefits by reducing the negative effects of constant connectivity, such as social isolation and mental health issues. Through thoughtful policy interventions, society can navigate the complexities of the digital age while promoting a more balanced and mindful relationship with technology.

Government initiatives supporting digital minimalism

In recent years, government initiatives have been introduced to support the adoption of digital minimalism as a means to promote mental well-being and productivity. From public awareness campaigns to policy changes, various actions have been taken to address the concerns surrounding excessive screen time and digital addiction. For example, some countries have implemented regulations that limit the use of smartphones in schools to protect students from distractions and promote face-to-face interactions. Additionally, government-sponsored programs have been launched to educate the public on the importance of practicing digital detox and unplugging from technology regularly. By recognizing the impact of technology on individuals' mental health and overall quality of life, these initiatives aim to empower people to take control of their digital habits and find a healthier balance between the virtual and real world. As society continues to grapple with the challenges posed by constant connectivity, governmental support for digital minimalism is crucial in fostering a more mindful and intentional use of technology.

Public campaigns and awareness programs

Public campaigns and awareness programs play a crucial role in promoting the benefits of digital minimalism and encouraging individuals to disconnect for a better life. These initiatives can educate the public about the negative impacts of excessive screen time on mental health, relationships, and overall well-being. By raising awareness through social media campaigns, workshops, and community events, more people can become informed about the importance of setting boundaries with technology. Additionally, public campaigns can provide tips and strategies for incorporating digital detoxes into one's routine, helping individuals cultivate healthier habits and reduce their reliance on screens. Ultimately, these efforts can empower individuals to take control of their digital usage, leading to better focus, improved relationships, and a greater sense of balance in their daily lives. By advocating for digital minimalism through public campaigns, we can create a culture that values mindful engagement with technology.

Policy challenges and solutions

One of the key policy challenges that arise in the context of digital minimalism is the need for regulatory frameworks to protect individuals' privacy and personal data. This issue has become increasingly important as technology companies amass vast amounts of user information, often without explicit consent. Governments must implement rigorous data protection laws and enforce them effectively to ensure that individuals have control over their digital footprint. Additionally, there is a growing need for policies that promote digital literacy and responsible technology use, especially among young people. Schools and educational institutions can play a crucial role in teaching students how to navigate the digital world thoughtfully and critically. By addressing these policy challenges, society can work towards creating a healthier and more balanced relationship with technology, fostering a culture of digital minimalism that prioritizes human well-being over constant connectivity.

XXVIII. TECHNOLOGY DEVELOPERS AND DIGITAL MINIMALISM

The landscape of technology developers is vast and ever-growing, with new innovations constantly being introduced to the market. As consumers, we are bombarded with a myriad of apps, gadgets, and platforms vying for our attention. However, the philosophy of digital minimalism offers an alternative approach to navigating this digital jungle. By consciously reducing our digital footprint and decluttering our online presence, we can reclaim our time and focus on what truly matters. Technology developers can play a crucial role in promoting digital minimalism by designing products that prioritize simplicity, functionality, and user well-being. Rather than succumbing to the pressure of constant connectivity and information overload, we can seek out tools that enable us to disconnect mindfully and cultivate a healthier relationship with technology. In a world where innovation often outpaces introspection, embracing digital minimalism can empower us to live more intentional and fulfilling lives.

Designing technology with minimalism in mind

In today's fast-paced world, designing technology with minimalism in mind has become crucial for ensuring that users can navigate digital spaces with ease and focus. By stripping away unnecessary features and distractions, minimalist technology allows individuals to engage more deeply with their tasks and goals without being overwhelmed by an overload of information. This intentional approach to design emphasizes clarity, simplicity, and functionality, which can lead to increased efficiency and productivity. Additionally, minimalistic technology promotes mindfulness and intentionality in users' digital interactions, encouraging them to be more conscious of how they spend their time online. By streamlining the user experience and minimizing clutter, designers can create digital tools that enhance users' well-being and help them achieve a better balance between their online and offline lives. Ultimately, incorporating minimalism into technology design can lead to a more harmonious relationship between individuals and their digital devices.

Ethical considerations for developers

When considering ethical considerations for developers in the context of digital minimalism, it is important to recognize the potential impact of their creations on individuals and society as a whole. Developers have a responsibility to prioritize user well-being over maximizing profit or engagement metrics. They must consider the ethical implications of their design choices, such as creating addictive features or exploiting users' data for targeted advertising. By upholding ethical standards, developers can contribute to a culture of digital mindfulness and promote healthier relationships with technology. Additionally, developers should prioritize user privacy and data security to protect individuals from potential harm. By adhering to ethical guidelines, developers can play a key role in shaping a more ethical and responsible digital landscape that prioritizes the well-being of users above all else.

Examples of minimalist tech products

In the realm of minimalist tech products, the Apple AirPods stand out as a prime example of sleek design and functionality.

With their wireless design, these earbuds eliminate the need for tangled cords and bulky headphones, allowing users to enjoy music and take calls with ease. Another minimalist tech product is the Kindle e-reader, which provides a simple and distraction-free reading experience. With its e-ink display and long battery life, the Kindle allows readers to immerse themselves in books without the distractions of notifications or other apps. Finally, the Nest Learning Thermostat embodies minimalist design with its intuitive interface and energy-saving features. By learning your habits and adjusting the temperature accordingly, the Nest Thermostat simplifies the process of controlling your home's climate. Overall, these examples of minimalist tech products demonstrate how simplicity and functionality can enhance our daily lives.

XXIX. DIGITAL MINIMALISM AND MEDIA CONSUMPTION

In the age of constant connectivity and digital bombardment, digital minimalism offers a refreshing antidote to the overwhelming noise of media consumption. By deliberately curating our online interactions and reducing mindless scrolling, digital minimalism encourages a more intentional and mindful approach to technology use. This concept advocates for a thoughtful evaluation of the role digital devices play in our lives, prompting us to prioritize quality over quantity when it comes to our online activities. Through the practice of digital minimalism, individuals can reclaim their time and attention, fostering deeper connections in both the virtual and real world. By disconnecting from the incessant pull of digital distractions, we can create space for reflection, creativity, and genuine human interaction. Ultimately, embracing digital minimalism can lead to a more balanced and fulfilling existence in our increasingly digital-centric world.

Altering media consumption habits

As individuals become increasingly aware of the negative effects of constant media consumption on their mental health and productivity, many are seeking ways to alter their habits for a more balanced lifestyle. By practicing digital minimalism, individuals can intentionally limit their exposure to distractions and mindless scrolling, allowing them to focus on more meaningful activities. This intentional approach to media consumption involves setting boundaries, such as designating specific times for checking social media or turning off notifications during work hours. Through this conscious effort to disconnect from the online world, individuals can reclaim their time and attention for activities that bring them genuine fulfillment and joy. Ultimately, by altering their media consumption habits, individuals can cultivate a healthier relationship with technology and improve their overall well-being.

Impact on news consumption and awareness

When considering the impact of digital minimalism on news consumption and awareness, it is evident that technology plays a significant role in shaping how individuals engage with information. With the rise of social media platforms and online news outlets, people are constantly bombarded with a barrage of headlines and updates that can lead to information overload and decreased critical thinking. However, by practicing digital minimalism and intentionally unplugging from these constant sources of information, individuals can regain control over their news consumption habits and cultivate a more mindful approach to staying informed. By limiting screen time and opting for more traditional sources of news, such as newspapers or podcasts, individuals can focus on quality over quantity, leading to a more informed and balanced perspective on current events. In this way, digital minimalism can empower individuals to curate their news consumption in a way that promotes greater awareness and critical thinking.

Media literacy in a minimalist digital world

In today's minimalist digital world, media literacy plays a crucial role in helping individuals navigate the vast ocean of information available online. As we strive to disconnect from the constant barrage of notifications and distractions, it is essential to develop a critical eye for the media we consume. By honing our media literacy skills, we can better discern between reliable sources and misinformation, filter out irrelevant content, and maintain control over our digital consumption habits. A minimalist approach to media consumption encourages us to be intentional about the content we engage with, allowing us to focus on what truly adds value to our lives. In this way, media literacy becomes a tool for empowerment, enabling us to make informed decisions about our digital interactions and ultimately leading to a more balanced and fulfilling life.

XXX. NETWORKING AND PROFESSIONAL RELATIONSHIPS

Networking and professional relationships play a crucial role in today's interconnected world. Building a strong network of contacts can open doors to new opportunities, whether it be career advancement, business partnerships, or collaborations on projects. By establishing meaningful connections with peers, mentors, and industry leaders, individuals can gain valuable insights, advice, and support that can propel their professional growth. Networking not only expands one's knowledge base but also enhances their visibility within their field, increasing the likelihood of being considered for new prospects. Additionally, cultivating professional relationships requires a blend of authenticity, reciprocity, and active participation. It is vital to engage with others genuinely, show appreciation for their contributions, and offer assistance when possible. Ultimately, investing time and effort into networking can yield substantial returns in terms of career success and personal development.

Networking without digital overload

In today's digital age, networking without being overwhelmed by the constant influx of information and notifications can be a daunting task. However, by embracing the principles of digital minimalism, individuals can create a more intentional approach to their online interactions. By prioritizing quality over quantity, individuals can focus on building meaningful connections with others. This can involve limiting the number of social media platforms one engages with, setting boundaries for when and how often to check emails, and being selective about the online communities one participates in. By decluttering their digital lives, individuals can create space for more meaningful interactions, leading to deeper relationships and increased productivity. Ultimately, networking without digital overload is about finding a balance that allows for genuine connections while reducing the distractions that can hinder personal and professional growth.

Maintaining professional relationships with minimal digital use

In today's digital age, it can be challenging to maintain professional relationships with minimal digital use. However, by setting boundaries and being intentional with our communication methods, it is possible to cultivate strong connections without relying heavily on technology. One effective strategy is to schedule regular face-to-face meetings or phone calls with colleagues or clients. This allows for more personal and meaningful interactions, fostering trust and rapport. Additionally, being mindful of our digital interactions by prioritizing quality over quantity can help us avoid the pitfalls of over-reliance on technology. By limiting the distractions of constant notifications and social media updates, we can focus on building genuine connections and fostering professional growth. Ultimately, finding a balance between digital communication and in-person interactions is key to maintaining professional relationships with minimal digital use and cultivating a more fulfilling work environment.

Case studies of networking in a minimalist digital environment

When exploring case studies of networking in a minimalist digital environment, we can observe the positive impacts of reducing screen time and embracing real-life connections. For example, studies have shown that individuals who limit their social media usage to a few select platforms or specific times of the day tend to have stronger relationships and a higher sense of well-being. By intentionally curating their online interactions and focusing on quality over quantity, these individuals are able to foster deeper connections with friends and family. Additionally, those who prioritize face-to-face interactions over virtual communication often experience increased levels of happiness and fulfillment. These case studies highlight the importance of creating boundaries and being mindful of how we engage with technology in order to cultivate more meaningful relationships and lead a more balanced life. By following their examples, we can learn to prioritize human connections and enrich our lives beyond the digital realm.

XXXI. DIGITAL MINIMALISM AND ARTISTIC EXPRESSION

Digital minimalism not only offers a path towards reducing distractions and reclaiming our attention, but it also holds profound implications for artistic expression. By disconnecting from the constant barrage of notifications and social media feeds, individuals can create the mental space necessary for deep, focused work. This intentional disconnection allows for a more profound engagement with the creative process, fostering a sense of mindfulness and presence that is essential for authentic artistic expression. Through digital minimalism, artists are able to cultivate a deeper connection to their inner thoughts and emotions, resulting in art that is more genuine and impactful. By stepping back from the digital world, individuals can tap into their creativity in a more meaningful way, leading to a richer and more fulfilling artistic practice. In this sense, digital minimalism not only benefits our daily lives but also enhances the quality and depth of our artistic endeavors.

Influence on the art world

The influence of digital minimalism on the art world is profound and multifaceted. Artists are increasingly turning to traditional mediums such as painting and sculpture as a way to disconnect from the digital realm and reconnect with their creative process on a more intimate level. This return to analog methods not only allows for a break from the constant distractions of technology but also fosters a deeper sense of mindfulness and authenticity in their work. Additionally, digital minimalism has spurred a new wave of minimalist art, characterized by simplicity, restraint,

103

and a focus on essential forms. This minimalist aesthetic not only reflects a desire for simplicity and clarity in a hyperconnected world but also challenges traditional notions of art and beauty. Overall, the impact of digital minimalism on the art world is reshaping artistic practices and aesthetic sensibilities in meaningful ways.

Artists embracing digital minimalism

In today's fast-paced digital world, many artists are embracing the concept of digital minimalism as a way to declutter their creative process and focus on what truly matters. By stripping away the distractions of constant connectivity and information overload, artists can tap into a deeper level of inspiration and creativity. Through intentional use of technology, they can curate their digital spaces to only include tools and resources that enhance their artistry, rather than detract from it. This newfound sense of simplicity allows artists to hone their craft, refine their artistic vision, and stay true to their creative instincts. Embracing digital minimalism not only helps artists to disconnect from the noise of the online world but also enables them to reconnect with their authentic selves and produce work that is both meaningful and impactful. By adopting a minimalist approach to their digital lives, artists can achieve a better balance between being connected and being present in the moment, ultimately leading to a more fulfilling and rewarding creative journey.

Impact on artistic creativity and production

The impact of digital minimalism on artistic creativity and production is profound. By disconnecting from the constant distractions of technology, individuals are able to tap into their true

104

creative potential. Without the interruptions of notifications, social media, and emails, artists can enter a state of flow where ideas can blossom freely and without restraint. This intentional disconnection allows for deep focus and immersive engagement with the creative process, resulting in more meaningful and innovative artistic output. Furthermore, digital minimalism encourages individuals to seek inspiration from the physical world around them, rather than relying solely on digital sources. This shift in perspective can lead to a richer and more authentic artistic expression. Overall, digital minimalism provides a fertile ground for artistic exploration and production, allowing creators to break free from the constraints of technology and unleash their full creative potential.

XXXII. RELIGIOUS AND SPIRITUAL PERSPECTIVES ON DIGITAL MINIMALISM

In the realm of religious and spiritual perspectives, digital minimalism offers a unique approach to finding balance in a technology-driven world. Many belief systems emphasize the importance of presence, mindfulness, and connection to the divine, values that can easily be overshadowed by constant digital distractions. By embracing digital minimalism, individuals can create space for deeper spiritual practices, whether it be through meditation, prayer, or simply being fully present in the moment. In a society where devices constantly vie for our attention, incorporating principles of minimalism can help individuals realign their priorities and focus on what truly matters in their spiritual journey. By disconnecting from the digital noise, individuals may find renewed clarity and a deeper connection to their faith, allowing for a more meaningful and intentional spiritual experience in the modern age.

Digital minimalism in religious practices

In today's digitally connected world, the concept of digital minimalism is gaining traction in various facets of life, including religious practices. In the context of religious observance, digital minimalism encourages individuals to disconnect from the constant barrage of notifications and distractions that technology brings, allowing for a more focused and intentional engagement with spiritual matters. By limiting the use of digital devices during religious rituals, individuals can create a sacred space free from interruptions and external influences, enabling a deeper connection with their faith. This practice promotes mindfulness, fosters a sense of reverence, and cultivates a greater sense of presence during religious ceremonies or meditative practices. Embracing digital minimalism in religious activities can not only enhance the spiritual experience but also promote a more profound sense of connection with oneself, the divine, and the community of believers.

Spiritual benefits of reduced digital use

In the quest for digital minimalism, one of the most significant benefits that emerge is the enhancement of spiritual well-being. By reducing excessive digital use, individuals can create more space for mindfulness, presence, and deep connections with themselves and others. Disconnecting from the constant barrage of notifications and distractions allows individuals to cultivate a sense of inner peace and clarity, fostering a deeper connection with their inner selves. This newfound mental clarity can lead to a greater sense of purpose and fulfillment in life, as individuals are able to prioritize what truly matters to them. Moreover, reduced digital use can provide opportunities for meaningful face-to-face interactions, fostering genuine relationships and a sense of community. In essence, embracing digital minimalism opens up a pathway to spiritual growth, enabling individuals to align their actions with their values and connect with the deeper aspects of their being.

Case studies from various religious communities

In exploring the impacts of digital minimalism on various religious communities, case studies offer valuable insights into how technology use can influence spiritual practices and beliefs. For example, studies have shown that digital distractions can hinder the depth of religious experiences and mindfulness in prayer among individuals in these communities. On the other hand, some religious groups have embraced digital minimalism as a means to cultivate a more intentional and focused spiritual life, using technology judiciously to enhance community connections and outreach efforts. By examining these diverse case studies, we can glean important lessons on the potential benefits and challenges of integrating technology into religious practices. Ultimately, these studies underscore the importance of mindful technology use in fostering a deeper connection to one's spiritual beliefs and community.

XXXIII. DIGITAL MINIMALISM AND GLOBAL CONNECTIVITY

In the age of global connectivity, where digital technology has become an integral part of our daily lives, the concept of digital minimalism has emerged as a compelling antidote to the overwhelming presence of screens and notifications. By embracing a minimalist approach to our digital consumption, we can cultivate a more intentional and mindful relationship with technology. This shift towards digital minimalism encourages us to prioritize quality over quantity, focusing on the meaningful connections and experiences that enrich our lives rather than getting lost in the endless scroll of social media feeds. In practicing digital minimalism, we reclaim control over our attention and time, allowing us to engage more deeply with the world around us and nurture genuine human connections. By disconnecting from the constant noise of the digital world, we create space for reflection, creativity, and genuine moments of presence in our increasingly fast-paced and tech-saturated society.

Balancing global connectivity with minimalism

In today's interconnected world, striking a balance between global connectivity and minimalism has become increasingly challenging. While technology has made it easier to stay connected with people and information from all around the world, it has also led to information overload and a constant sense of being plugged in. Digital minimalism offers a solution to this dilemma by encouraging individuals to evaluate their digital consumption habits and prioritize quality over quantity. By intentionally choosing which platforms and devices to engage with, one can minimize distractions and focus on what truly matters. This approach not only promotes mental clarity and productivity but also fosters a deeper sense of connection with oneself and others. Embracing digital minimalism empowers individuals to cultivate a more mindful and intentional relationship with technology, allowing them to reap the benefits of global connectivity while minimizing its negative impacts on their well-being.

Impact on international relations and understanding

One significant impact of digital minimalism on international relations and understanding is the cultivation of a more authentic and meaningful global dialogue. By disconnecting from the constant barrage of information and distractions that digital devices offer, individuals are able to engage in more mindful and intentional communication with others from different cultures and backgrounds. This deliberate approach to interaction helps to foster empathy, understanding, and respect for diverse perspectives, ultimately strengthening relationships on an international scale. Additionally, the practice of digital minimalism encourages individuals to seek out face-to-face interactions and genuine connections, which can transcend linguistic and cultural barriers. As a result, digital minimalism has the potential to bridge gaps in understanding between people from different parts of the world, paving the way for more harmonious and cooperative relationships on a global level.

Case studies of global initiatives

In exploring case studies of global initiatives that promote digital minimalism, it is evident that various organizations and individuals are recognizing the importance of disconnecting from technology to improve overall well-being. For example, the Slow Tech Movement, which originated in Europe, encourages individuals to reduce their reliance on digital devices and embrace a simpler, more intentional way of living. Through workshops, retreats, and community events, this initiative promotes mindfulness and the value of unplugging in a hyper-connected world. Additionally, the Digital Detox organization in the United States offers retreats where participants can engage in offline activities such as hiking, art workshops, and yoga, fostering face-to-face connections and real-life experiences. These case studies highlight the growing trend of individuals seeking to regain control over their digital habits and prioritize more meaningful interactions in a technology-saturated society.

XXXIV. DIGITAL MINIMALISM AND URBAN LIVING

As urban living becomes increasingly synonymous with the fast-paced, connected nature of the digital age, the concept of digital minimalism offers a refreshing perspective on how individuals can navigate this bustling environment. By embracing the principles of digital minimalism, individuals can intentionally curate their relationship with technology, allowing them to prioritize present-moment experiences and meaningful connections in their urban surroundings. As cities become hubs of constant digital stimuli, practicing digital minimalism can serve as a powerful tool to cultivate mindfulness, reduce distractions, and cultivate a sense of balance in one's daily life. Instead of being overwhelmed by the incessant demands of technology in urban settings, individuals can leverage digital minimalism to reclaim agency over their attention and time, fostering a more intentional and fulfilling experience amidst the hustle and bustle of city living.

Challenges and strategies in urban environments

Urban environments pose a myriad of challenges that can hinder individuals' well-being and productivity. Issues such as overcrowding, pollution, limited green spaces, and high levels of noise can contribute to stress and diminish the overall quality of life in these settings. To combat these challenges, urban dwellers can implement various strategies. One effective approach is to prioritize green spaces and create urban gardens or parks that provide a respite from the concrete jungle. Additionally, investing in public transportation and promoting walkability can help reduce congestion and pollution levels. Embracing technology to improve urban planning and resource management can also lead to more sustainable and efficient living environments. By addressing these challenges with innovative solutions, urban areas can become more livable, healthier, and ultimately more conducive to overall well-being.

Impact on city planning and community living

In the realm of city planning and community living, the rise of digital minimalism has had a profound impact on how urban spaces are designed and utilized. With the increasing emphasis on disconnecting from constant digital distractions, city planners are now incorporating more green spaces, pedestrian-friendly areas, and communal gathering spots into their designs. This shift in focus from technology-driven to human-centered urban planning has resulted in more cohesive and livable communities where people can engage in face-to-face interactions and enjoy the outdoors. By encouraging a minimalist approach to technology use, city dwellers are able to foster stronger social connections, promote mental well-being, and reduce the feelings of isolation that often accompany excessive screen time. Ultimately, the integration of digital minimalism principles into city planning endeavors has the potential to create more vibrant and sustainable urban environments that prioritize human interaction and community living.

Urban versus rural digital minimalism

In considering digital minimalism in urban versus rural settings, it is evident that the impact of technology on daily life varies greatly depending on the environment. Urban areas are often characterized by a fast-paced lifestyle, where individuals are constantly bombarded by digital distractions and the need to always be connected. In this setting, the practice of digital minimalism may be more challenging but also more necessary to maintain a sense of balance and mental well-being. On the other hand, rural areas typically offer a slower pace of life and a closer connection to nature, which may naturally lend themselves to a more minimalist approach to technology use. However, rural areas can also face challenges such as limited access to high-speed internet, which may necessitate a different approach to digital minimalism. Ultimately, whether in urban or rural environments, the principles of digital minimalism can help individuals navigate the complexities of modern technology and find a healthier balance in their lives.

XXXV. DIGITAL MINIMALISM AND CRISIS MANAGEMENT

In times of crisis, the principles of digital minimalism can be a powerful tool for managing stress and maintaining mental clarity. When faced with overwhelming situations, the constant barrage of notifications and distractions from our digital devices can exacerbate feelings of anxiety and reduce our ability to focus on important tasks. By adopting a digital minimalist approach during times of crisis, individuals can intentionally limit their use of technology to essential functions, such as communication with loved ones or accessing critical information. This intentional disconnection from the noise of the digital world can create space for reflection, deep thinking, and self-care, all of which are crucial for effectively navigating challenging circumstances. Digital minimalism can serve as a shield against the constant demands of the virtual realm, allowing individuals to prioritize their mental well-being and focus on what truly matters in times of need.

Role during emergencies and crises

In times of emergencies and crises, the role of digital minimalism becomes increasingly prominent. As individuals are faced with overwhelming amounts of information and news updates, it can be easy to succumb to information overload and heightened anxiety levels. By practicing digital minimalism, individuals can intentionally disconnect from the constant barrage of notifications and headlines, allowing them to focus on the most essential information and take necessary actions. This deliberate choice to limit one's digital consumption can also create a sense of mental clarity and calmness during turbulent times, enabling individuals to make more informed decisions and prioritize their well-being. In essence, digital minimalism serves as a valuable tool for maintaining a balanced and healthy mindset amidst chaos and uncertainty, helping individuals navigate through emergencies with greater resilience and focus.

Strategies for minimal digital use in critical times

In critical times, when digital overload can lead to increased stress and anxiety, it is essential to develop strategies for minimal digital use. One effective approach is setting clear boundaries for technology usage, such as allocating specific times during the day for checking emails or social media. By creating designated periods for digital interaction, individuals can ensure that technology does not encroach on other important aspects of their lives, such as work or personal relationships. Another strategy is to prioritize face-to-face interactions over digital communication whenever possible. By choosing to engage in direct, in-person conversations, individuals can foster deeper connections and avoid the pitfalls of miscommunication that often arise in digital exchanges. Ultimately, by implementing these strategies for minimal digital use, individuals can create a healthier balance between their online and offline lives, leading to increased focus, productivity, and overall well-being.

Case studies of crisis management with minimal digital interference

A notable case study of crisis management with minimal digital interference is the response to the 1982 Tylenol poisonings.

When several people died after ingesting cyanide-laced capsules of Tylenol, Johnson & Johnson immediately took action by recalling over 31 million bottles of the product, costing the company millions of dollars. This swift and decisive response not only demonstrated a commitment to customer safety but also showcased effective crisis management without the need for digital tools and platforms. By prioritizing public safety over potential financial losses, Johnson & Johnson was able to regain consumer trust and maintain their reputation as a responsible and ethical company. This case study serves as a powerful example of how companies can successfully navigate crises without relying heavily on digital communication channels, highlighting the importance of clear communication, quick decision-making, and a focus on human connections in times of crisis.

XXXVI. DIGITAL MINIMALISM AND LIFESTYLE BRANDS

Digital minimalism, characterized by intentional use of technology to enhance well-being, can intersect with lifestyle brands that promote simplicity and mindfulness. These brands cater to individuals seeking to declutter their lives and prioritize meaningful experiences over material possessions. By embracing digital minimalism, individuals can align their online presence with their values, curating a digital environment that reflects their authentic selves. Lifestyle brands can play a significant role in guiding consumers towards a more intentional and mindful way of living, encouraging them to disconnect from the constant digital stimulus and cultivate a deeper connection with the world around them. As such, the marriage of digital minimalism and lifestyle brands can empower individuals to make conscious choices about how they engage with technology and shape their overall lifestyle, ultimately leading to a more balanced and fulfilling existence.

Influence on lifestyle brand strategies

Lifestyle brand strategies are significantly influenced by the concept of digital minimalism. In today's digital age, consumers are inundated with endless choices and distractions, leading them to seek simplicity and authenticity in their lives. As a result, brands are increasingly focusing on promoting minimalist lifestyles to connect with their target audiences. By aligning their values and messages with the principles of digital minimalism, brands can attract consumers who are seeking balance and mindfulness in a chaotic world. Embracing minimalism in their marketing strategies allows brands to stand out in a cluttered marketplace and build a strong emotional connection with their customers. Moreover, by promoting a simpler and more mindful way of living, brands can help consumers prioritize what truly matters to them, leading to a more meaningful and fulfilling lifestyle. Ultimately, digital minimalism can guide lifestyle brands in creating authentic and resonant messages that resonate with today's conscious consumers.

Brand adaptations to the minimalist digital trend

In response to the growing popularity of digital minimalism, many brands are adapting their strategies to align with this trend. One way in which brands are adjusting is by simplifying their product offerings and messaging to resonate with the minimalist ethos. By focusing on quality over quantity and offering streamlined, clutter-free designs, brands are able to appeal to consumers who are seeking a more minimalist lifestyle. Additionally, many brands are prioritizing sustainability and ethical practices in response to the environmental concerns raised by digital minimalists. By reducing waste and promoting responsible consumption, these brands are able to appeal to a growing segment of the population that is seeking to minimize their impact on the planet. Overall, brand adaptations to the minimalist digital trend are not only reflective of changing consumer preferences but also demonstrate a commitment to social and environmental responsibility in the modern marketplace.

Consumer response to minimalist branding

The consumer response to minimalist branding within the digital realm is a fascinating phenomenon that highlights a shift towards simplicity and authenticity in today's fast-paced society. As individuals become increasingly bombarded with information and stimuli online, minimalist branding offers a breath of fresh air by providing clean and uncluttered designs that convey a sense of sophistication and elegance. This approach resonates with consumers who are seeking a more streamlined and uncomplicated lifestyle, free from unnecessary distractions. By embracing minimalist branding, companies can tap into this desire for simplicity and position themselves as purveyors of refined taste and sophistication. This consumer response underscores the power of minimalist branding in capturing the attention and loyalty of modern audiences who value quality over quantity and seek meaningful connections in a digital landscape filled with noise and clutter.

XXXVII. DIGITAL MINIMALISM AND TRAVEL

In the realm of travel, embracing digital minimalism can lead to a more enriching and authentic experience. By consciously reducing the time spent on devices, travelers can be fully present in their surroundings, immersing themselves in the culture, sights, and sounds of a new destination. Disconnecting from the constant stream of notifications and social media updates allows individuals to engage more deeply with the local community, forming genuine connections and creating lasting memories. Moreover, digital minimalism in travel promotes mindfulness and self-reflection, enabling individuals to appreciate the beauty of the moment without the distractions of technology. Whether embarking on a solo adventure or traveling with loved ones, adopting a minimalist approach to digital consumption can transform a trip into a transformative and meaningful journey. By prioritizing real-life experiences over virtual ones, travelers can cultivate a sense of fulfillment and connection that extends far beyond the confines of a screen.

Enhancing travel experiences through minimal digital use

Digital minimalism offers a unique approach to enhancing travel experiences by encouraging individuals to disconnect from excessive digital use. By limiting screen time and focusing on being present in the moment, travelers can fully immerse themselves in their surroundings, engage with the local culture, and create lasting memories. Embracing minimal digital use can also lead to a more authentic and meaningful travel experience, free from distractions and preoccupation with virtual connections. Instead of relying on technology for directions or recommendations, travelers can tap into their own intuition, interact with locals, and stumble upon hidden gems that may have been overlooked in a digital-centric travel approach. Ultimately, by disconnecting from the digital world, travelers can connect more deeply with themselves, their surroundings, and the experiences that make travel truly enriching.

Travel industry adaptations to digital minimalism

In response to the growing trend of digital minimalism, the travel industry has been forced to adapt to meet the changing needs and preferences of consumers. One notable adaptation has been the rise of "unplugged" travel experiences, where tourists are encouraged to disconnect from their devices and immerse themselves fully in the destination. This shift towards digital detox vacations highlights a desire for authentic, meaningful experiences that prioritize human connection and presence over constant connectivity. Additionally, travel companies have started to offer tech-free zones, where guests can unwind without the distractions of screens and notifications. By catering to the increasing demand for digital minimalism in travel, companies are not only staying relevant in a rapidly changing market but also providing a much-needed escape from the digital overload plaguing modern society. This shift towards more mindful travel experiences showcases the powerful impact of digital minimalism on shaping industries beyond just technology.

Case studies of minimalist travel experiences

One compelling case study of minimalist travel experiences involves the concept of "backpacking light," where travelers opt for a streamlined approach to packing and living on the road. By carrying only the essentials in a single backpack, these individuals embrace a minimalist mindset that prioritizes mobility and simplicity. This approach not only reduces the physical weight of belongings but also fosters a sense of liberation from material possessions, allowing travelers to focus more on the experiences and connections they encounter along the way. Through challenging the conventional norms of travel, minimalist backpackers demonstrate how embracing simplicity can lead to a more enriching and fulfilling journey. By shedding the excess, they create space for meaningful interactions, personal growth, and a deeper appreciation for the world around them. Ultimately, these case studies highlight the transformative power of minimalism in enhancing the travel experience and fostering a greater sense of connection to the people and places encountered on the road.

XXXVIII. DIGITAL MINIMALISM AND RETIREMENT

As individuals enter the stage of retirement, the concept of digital minimalism can play a crucial role in helping them navigate this new phase of life. By embracing a minimalist approach to technology use, retirees can cultivate a sense of mindfulness and intentionality in their day-to-day activities. This deliberate choice to limit digital distractions can lead to deeper connections with loved ones, increased engagement in hobbies and interests, and a greater appreciation for the present moment. In retirement, where time becomes a precious commodity, digital minimalism allows individuals to focus on what truly matters to them, fostering a sense of fulfillment and contentment in this new chapter of life. By disconnecting from the constant stream of notifications and information overload, retirees can create a more peaceful and meaningful existence, free from the pressures of always being connected.

Adapting digital minimalism for retirees

As retirees enter a phase of life characterized by increased leisure time and reduced professional responsibilities, they may find themselves grappling with how best to navigate the digital landscape that has become so pervasive in modern society. Adapting the principles of digital minimalism can offer retirees a sense of control over their technology use, allowing them to focus on meaningful activities and connections that enhance their well-being. By intentionally curating their digital footprint, retirees can create a more intentional and fulfilling retirement experience. This may involve setting boundaries around screen time, decluttering digital spaces to create a more serene environment, and prioritizing face-to-face interactions over virtual communication. Embracing digital minimalism can empower retirees to reclaim their time and attention, leading to a more enriching and purposeful post-career life.

Benefits for the elderly

In addition to the benefits for mental health and productivity, digital minimalism can also have significant advantages for the elderly. As individuals age, they may find themselves overwhelmed by the constant influx of information and stimuli from the digital world. By practicing digital minimalism, older adults can reduce cognitive overload and improve their focus and attention span. This can be particularly beneficial for those facing age-related cognitive decline or memory issues. Furthermore, disconnecting from digital devices allows seniors to spend more quality time engaging in activities that promote social connections, physical activity, and mental stimulation. By prioritizing real-world interactions and hobbies over screen time, the elderly can foster stronger relationships, maintain a sense of purpose, and lead a more fulfilling and active lifestyle in their later years. Overall, digital minimalism offers a holistic approach to well-being that is especially valuable for older individuals looking to enhance their overall quality of life.

Community programs supporting elderly digital minimalism

In response to the growing trend of digital minimalism among the elderly population, community programs are emerging to support and empower seniors in navigating the digital world while maintaining a healthy balance. These programs offer workshops, seminars, and one-on-one coaching sessions to teach older adults how to streamline their digital devices, declutter their online presence, and prioritize meaningful interactions over mindless scrolling. By fostering a sense of community and providing personalized guidance, these initiatives help seniors feel more confident and in control of their digital habits. Additionally, these programs encourage social engagement and peer support, combating the isolation that some older adults may experience in this increasingly interconnected world. Overall, community programs supporting elderly digital minimalism play a crucial role in promoting mental well-being, fostering a sense of belonging, and empowering older individuals to lead fulfilling and intentional lives in the digital age.

XXXIX. DIGITAL MINIMALISM AND PARENTING

As parents navigate the challenges of raising children in a digitally saturated world, the principles of digital minimalism can offer valuable insight into establishing healthy boundaries and promoting mindful technology use within the family unit. By prioritizing face-to-face interactions and fostering offline hobbies and activities, parents can model a balanced approach to technology that encourages children to develop strong social skills, focus, and creativity. Setting limits on screen time, implementing tech-free zones in the home, and engaging in open discussions about the impact of digital devices on well-being are effective strategies for instilling a sense of mindfulness and intentionality in both children and parents alike. Through practicing digital minimalism in parenting, families can cultivate deeper connections, promote mental health, and foster a more harmonious relationship with technology in the modern age.

Strategies for raising children with minimal digital exposure

In a world saturated with digital devices and constant connectivity, raising children with minimal digital exposure can be a challenging but beneficial endeavor. Parents can employ several strategies to limit their children's screen time and encourage alternative forms of entertainment and engagement. Implementing strict screen-time rules, setting boundaries by establishing tech-free zones in the house, and promoting outdoor activities or creative hobbies are effective ways to reduce children's reliance on screens. Additionally, fostering meaningful face-to-face interactions, encouraging reading, and modeling mindful technology use can shape children's attitudes towards digital devices. By prioritizing quality time spent together as a family and emphasizing the importance of balance in technology consumption, parents can create a healthy environment that supports their children's overall well-being and development. Ultimately, adopting a mindful and intentional approach to digital exposure can help children cultivate essential life skills and habits that will serve them well in the long run.

Impact on family dynamics and communication

Digital minimalism has the potential to significantly impact family dynamics and communication within households. By limiting screen time and focusing on real-world interactions, families can strengthen their bonds and create deeper connections. This shift away from constant digital distractions allows for more meaningful conversations and quality time spent together. Parents who practice digital minimalism set a positive example for their children, encouraging them to engage in activities that promote growth and development. Shared experiences such as game nights, outdoor adventures, or even just sitting together without devices can foster better communication skills and foster stronger relationships. In this way, digital minimalism can reshape the way families interact and communicate, ultimately leading to healthier and more fulfilling relationships.

Parental guidance and support systems

In the realm of digital minimalism, parental guidance and support systems play a crucial role in shaping how individuals navigate their relationship with technology. Parents who set boundaries and model healthy behavior around screen time can instill valuable habits in their children from a young age. By empha-sizing the importance of offline activities, face-to-face interac-tions, and limiting screen time, parents can help their children develop a balanced approach to technology use. Moreover, sup-port systems that offer guidance and resources for parents nav-igating the digital landscape can be instrumental in fostering a mindful approach to technology use within the family unit. These systems can provide valuable insights, strategies, and support networks for parents looking to create a healthy digital environ-ment for their children. Ultimately, parental guidance and sup-port systems are essential components in promoting digital well-being and instilling a sense of balance in an increasingly digital world.

XL. DIGITAL MINIMALISM AND FITNESS

When it comes to incorporating digital minimalism into our daily routines, the realm of fitness presents a unique opportunity for us to detach from the constant distractions of technology. Embracing a more minimalist approach to our digital devices can allow us to focus more fully on our physical well-being, whether it be through engaging in outdoor activities, attending fitness classes, or simply finding time for solitude and self-reflection. By disconnecting from the constant notifications and screens that often consume our attention, we can better tune into our bodies, minds, and environments, creating a more mindful and intentional approach to our fitness goals. This intentional disconnection can not only lead to improved physical health but also promote mental clarity and emotional well-being. Ultimately, integrating digital minimalism into our fitness routines can help us cultivate a more balanced and holistic approach to overall wellness in an increasingly digital world.

Integrating physical fitness with digital minimalism

In today's fast-paced digital age, integrating physical fitness with digital minimalism has become essential for maintaining a healthy balance in our lives. By combining the benefits of staying active with the principles of reducing screen time and online distractions, individuals can experience a more holistic approach to overall well-being. Engaging in physical exercise not only helps to improve physical health but also boosts mental clarity and focus, which are crucial components of digital minimalism. By incorporating regular workouts or outdoor activities into our daily routines, we can disconnect from the constant digital noise and reconnect with ourselves and the physical world around us. This integration fosters a more mindful and intentional use of technology, allowing us to prioritize our health and wellness while still enjoying the benefits of digital tools and connectivity. In essence, the synergy between physical fitness and digital minimalism offers a balanced approach to navigating the complexities of modern life.

Fitness industry responses to the minimalist trend

As the minimalist trend gains traction in various aspects of life, including the digital realm, the fitness industry has not been immune to its influence. Many fitness brands have started to embrace minimalist designs for their equipment, workout spaces, and apparel, reflecting a shift towards simplicity and functionality. This response to the minimalist trend is not just aesthetic; it also speaks to a deeper philosophy of focusing on essential movements and exercises that deliver results without unnecessary complexity. By stripping away distractions and unnecessary features, fitness companies are providing consumers with tools and environments that promote mindfulness, efficiency, and sustainability in their workout routines. This minimalist approach challenges the notion that more is always better, encouraging individuals to prioritize quality over quantity in their fitness pursuits. Overall, the fitness industry's response to the minimalist trend reflects a growing awareness of the benefits of simplicity and intentionality in promoting physical well-being.

Personal fitness stories related to minimal digital use

When considering personal fitness stories related to minimal

131

digital use, it becomes evident that disconnecting from technology can have a significant impact on one's physical well-being. Individuals who have successfully integrated digital minimalism into their daily routines often report a heightened sense of mindfulness and awareness of their bodies. With reduced screen time, these individuals have more time to engage in physical activities such as going for a run, practicing yoga, or hitting the gym. By prioritizing real-world experiences over virtual ones, they are able to improve their overall fitness levels and mental clarity. Moreover, limiting digital distractions allows individuals to focus more on their workouts, leading to better performance and results. As a result, personal fitness stories demonstrate the positive effects of minimal digital use on both physical health and mental well-being.

XLI. DIGITAL MINIMALISM AND NUTRITION

In the context of digital minimalism, the relationship between technology and nutrition is often overlooked but holds significant implications for our overall well-being. With the pervasive use of smartphones and other digital devices, many individuals find themselves mindlessly scrolling through social media feeds or watching endless videos, leading to a decrease in mindful eating practices. This behavior can result in overeating or consuming unhealthy foods as distractions take precedence over listening to our body's hunger cues. By practicing digital minimalism, we can create more intentional spaces for meal times, focusing on nourishing our bodies with wholesome foods and savoring the eating experience. Additionally, disconnecting from screens during meals allows for more meaningful connections with others, fostering a sense of community and support in maintaining healthy eating habits. Ultimately, embracing digital minimalism can lead to a more balanced relationship with food and technology, promoting overall wellness in our lives.

Influence on eating habits and food choices

In today's digital age, technology influences our eating habits and food choices in various ways. The accessibility of food delivery apps and online grocery shopping services has made it easier for individuals to order meals and snacks at the touch of a button, leading to an increase in convenient, but often less healthy, food options. Social media platforms are also influential in shaping our perceptions of food, with visually appealing images and influencers promoting certain diets or food trends. These digital platforms can create unrealistic standards of beauty and health, potentially leading to disordered eating habits. Additionally, the constant bombardment of advertisements for fast food and sugary snacks on websites and social media can tempt individuals to make impulsive food choices. As we navigate the digital landscape, it is essential to be mindful of how technology can impact our relationship with food and strive to make informed, balanced choices for our overall well-being.

Nutritional awareness in the digital minimalist lifestyle

In the digital minimalist lifestyle, where individuals aim to reduce screen time and online distractions, maintaining awareness of nutritional needs becomes even more crucial. With fewer opportunities for face-to-face interactions and physical activities, relying on digital resources for health-related information is common. However, this abundance of information can lead to misinformation and confusion about what constitutes a balanced diet. Therefore, it is essential for individuals practicing digital minimalism to cultivate a keen sense of nutritional awareness. This involves being mindful of food choices, understanding the importance of nutrients, and making conscious decisions about what goes into their bodies. By prioritizing nutritional awareness in conjunction with a minimalist approach to technology usage, individuals can enhance their overall well-being and lead healthier lifestyles in the digital age.

Integrating nutrition education with minimal digital usage

In the modern age of technology, it has become increasingly

challenging to maintain a healthy lifestyle and balanced nutrition habits while constantly being bombarded with digital distractions. However, by integrating nutrition education with minimal digital usage, individuals can cultivate a more mindful approach to their dietary choices. This can involve utilizing traditional methods of learning such as cookbooks, attending in-person nutrition workshops, and engaging in hands-on cooking classes. By reducing screen time and immersing oneself in these more tangible forms of education, individuals can deepen their understanding of nutrition and develop practical skills for meal planning and preparation. This intentional shift away from digital dependency can foster a stronger connection to food and promote overall well-being. Ultimately, embracing a lifestyle that prioritizes nutrition education over excessive screen time can lead to improved dietary habits and a healthier relationship with food.

XLII. DIGITAL MINIMALISM AND PERSONAL FINANCE

As individuals strive to adopt a lifestyle of digital minimalism, their approach to personal finance undergoes a significant transformation. By disconnecting from the constant bombardment of digital advertisements and notifications, individuals are better able to focus on their financial goals and priorities. Digital minimalism encourages mindfulness in spending, prompting individuals to evaluate their purchases more critically and avoid succumbing to impulse buys fueled by online advertising. This intentional approach to consumption not only leads to a more disciplined financial outlook but also cultivates a sense of contentment and fulfillment with one's belongings. As individuals embrace a simpler and more intentional lifestyle, they often find that their financial well-being improves, with increased savings and a reduced reliance on material possessions for happiness. Ultimately, digital minimalism and personal finance are intertwined in a symbiotic relationship, with each concept reinforcing the other to promote financial stability and a more meaningful existence.

Managing finances with minimal digital tools

In today's technologically driven world, managing finances with minimal digital tools may seem like a daunting task. However, it is possible to maintain control over your finances without relying heavily on digital platforms. One effective way to do this is by adopting a more traditional approach to managing money, such as using cash for transactions instead of relying on credit or debit cards. By physically seeing and handling money, individuals are more likely to be mindful of their spending habits and make conscious decisions about their purchases. Additionally, keeping track of expenses using a simple notebook or budgeting journal can help individuals stay organized and aware of their financial situation without the need for complex digital tools. While digital tools can offer convenience and efficiency, embracing a more hands-on approach to financial management can promote a deeper sense of financial responsibility and awareness.

Financial planning and advice for digital minimalists

Financial planning and advice for digital minimalists is essential in today's technology-driven world. By embracing a minimalist approach to digital consumption, individuals can reduce unnecessary spending on digital subscriptions, gadgets, and apps. One key aspect of financial planning for digital minimalists is creating a budget that prioritizes essential tech tools while cutting out non-essential expenses. This could involve evaluating current subscriptions and services to determine which ones truly add value to one's life. Additionally, setting financial goals and tracking progress can help digital minimalists stay on track with their spending and savings targets. Seeking advice from financial experts or utilizing budgeting apps can also provide valuable guidance and support for those looking to improve their financial health while practicing digital minimalism. Overall, integrating financial planning strategies into a digital minimalist lifestyle can lead to greater financial stability, mindfulness, and overall well-being.

Economic benefits of adopting a minimalist digital lifestyle

One of the key advantages of embracing a minimalist digital lifestyle is the potential for economic benefits. By reducing the time spent on digital devices, individuals can save money on expensive gadgets, data plans, apps, and subscriptions. In a world where the latest technology is constantly being marketed as essential, embracing digital minimalism can help individuals resist the urge to constantly upgrade to the newest model or purchase unnecessary digital products. Additionally, reducing screen time can lead to increased productivity and efficiency, allowing individuals to focus on more meaningful tasks that can lead to financial gains. By prioritizing real-life experiences over virtual ones, individuals can also save money on activities that cost money to participate in, ultimately leading to a more mindful approach towards spending and budgeting. Overall, adopting a minimalist digital lifestyle can not only lead to personal growth and well-being but also help individuals save money and make smarter financial decisions.

XLIII. DIGITAL MINIMALISM AND THE ARTS

The intersection of digital minimalism and the arts offers a unique perspective on how technology impacts creativity and artistic expression. By embracing a minimalist approach to digital consumption, artists can reclaim their focus, allowing for deeper immersion in the creative process. The constant distractions of digital devices can hinder the artistic flow, leading to superficial and fragmented works. Minimalism encourages artists to disconnect from the incessant noise of notifications and social media, creating space for introspection and genuine inspiration. This intentional disconnection can foster a more authentic and meaningful connection to one's craft, enabling artists to produce work that is truly reflective of their inner thoughts and emotions. Through digital minimalism, artists can cultivate a sense of mindfulness and presence in their artistic practice, ultimately leading to a more fulfilling and enriching creative experience.

Impact on various art forms

Digital minimalism has had a profound impact on various art forms, challenging traditional modes of creation and consumption. In the realm of visual arts, artists are exploring ways to use technology more intentionally, opting for analog methods or limiting their use of digital tools. This shift has led to a resurgence of interest in traditional art forms such as painting and sculpture, as artists seek to disconnect from the constant distractions of the digital world. Similarly, in music, there is a growing movement towards creating authentic, stripped-down compositions that eschew the overproduction often associated with digital music. This return to simplicity and mindfulness in art is a testament to the power of digital minimalism to inspire a more intentional and meaningful creative process, one that prioritizes human connection and emotional depth over technological bells and whistles.

Promoting traditional arts in a digital world

In a digital world dominated by technology and constant connectivity, promoting traditional arts may seem like a daunting task. However, the preservation and celebration of traditional arts are crucial for maintaining cultural heritage and identity in a rapidly changing society. By integrating traditional arts into the digital realm, we can reach a wider audience and ensure that these art forms are not lost to obscurity. Platforms such as social media, websites, and online galleries provide opportunities to showcase traditional arts to a global audience, sparking interest and appreciation for these time-honored crafts. Embracing digital tools can enhance the accessibility and visibility of traditional arts, attracting younger generations who are more accustomed to navigating the online landscape. Ultimately, promoting traditional arts in a digital world allows us to bridge the gap between the past and the present, ensuring that these valuable cultural expressions continue to thrive and resonate with contemporary audiences.

Artistic communities embracing minimalism

Artistic communities have long been at the forefront of embracing minimalism as a design aesthetic, emphasizing simplicity, clean lines, and a focus on essential elements. In the realm of visual arts, artists such as Donald Judd and Agnes Martin have championed minimalist principles, stripping away excess to reveal the pure essence of form and color. This minimalist approach has also found a home in other creative spheres, from music to architecture. By paring down to the essential components, artistic communities are able to create work that is not only visually striking but also carries a powerful sense of clarity and intention. Embracing minimalism allows artists to break free from the noise and distractions of a cluttered world, fostering a deeper connection between creator and audience. Ultimately, minimalism in art serves as a powerful reminder of the beauty and impact of simplicity in a complex and chaotic world.

XLIV. DIGITAL MINIMALISM AND SCIENCE

Digital minimalism is not just a personal lifestyle choice but has profound implications for science and research. In the age of information overload, the ability to disconnect and focus on what truly matters is becoming increasingly valuable. By embracing digital minimalism, scientists can enhance their productivity, creativity, and overall well-being. A clutter-free digital environment allows for deeper concentration, leading to more innovative and insightful discoveries. Moreover, limiting exposure to distractions and notifications can improve mental clarity and reduce stress, which are essential for optimal cognitive function in the scientific field. Embracing digital minimalism can lead to a more intentional and fulfilling scientific practice, where researchers can devote their energy to meaningful projects with a clear sense of purpose. In this way, digital minimalism goes beyond personal lifestyle choices and has the potential to revolutionize the way we approach scientific inquiry.

Scientific research on the benefits of digital minimalism

Digital minimalism has garnered attention in recent years as a potential solution to the negative impacts of excessive screen time and digital distractions. Scientific research has provided evidence to support the benefits of adopting a minimalist approach to technology use. Studies have shown that reducing screen time can lead to improved focus, mental clarity, and overall well-being. By limiting digital distractions, individuals can create more meaningful connections with others, enhance productivity, and improve their mental health. Digital minimalism encourages individuals to prioritize real-life experiences and relationships over virtual interactions, leading to a greater sense of fulfillment and satisfaction. Through intentional use of technology and a conscious effort to disconnect from mindless scrolling and constant notifications, individuals can reclaim their time and attention for activities that truly matter. Overall, scientific research supports the idea that digital minimalism can offer numerous benefits for individuals seeking a healthier and more balanced lifestyle.

Integration of minimal digital tools in scientific work

In the realm of scientific work, the integration of minimal digital tools can offer numerous benefits. By adopting a minimalist approach to technology, researchers can streamline their workflow, minimize distractions, and improve overall focus and productivity. With the rise of digital platforms and tools, it is crucial for scientists to carefully curate their digital environments to optimize their work processes. By embracing simplicity and efficiency in the use of technology, scientists can enhance the quality of their research and data analysis. Additionally, minimal digital tools can help researchers maintain a healthy balance between work and personal life, reducing the risk of burnout and improving overall well-being. In this fast-paced digital age, the integration of minimal digital tools in scientific work is not only practical but essential for cultivating a productive and fulfilling career in academia.

Case studies from the scientific community

Furthermore, case studies from the scientific community provide valuable insights into the benefits of embracing digital minimalism. Researchers have found that reducing screen time and unplugging from constant connectivity can lead to improved cognitive function, better sleep quality, and enhanced overall well-being. For example, a study published in the Journal of Experimental Psychology demonstrated that participants who spent less time on their phones experienced increased attention span and improved memory retention. Another study conducted by the National Sleep Foundation revealed that individuals who limited their screen time before bed reported falling asleep faster and experiencing longer periods of deep sleep. By examining these case studies, it becomes evident that adopting a minimalist approach to technology usage can have profound positive effects on both mental and physical health. As such, integrating principles of digital minimalism into daily routines can lead to a more balanced and fulfilling life.

XLV. DIGITAL MINIMALISM AND LITERATURE

Digital minimalism, as a lifestyle choice, has profound implications for the world of literature. By disconnecting from the constant barrage of digital distractions, individuals can reclaim their attention and focus on engaging with the written word in a more meaningful way. This shift towards minimalism allows for a return to the deliberate and immersive reading experience that is often lost in the age of smartphones and social media. When we prioritize quality over quantity in our digital interactions, we create space for literature to once again hold a central place in our lives. This intentional curation of our digital consumption opens up opportunities for deeper engagement with texts, fostering critical thinking and reflection. In essence, digital minimalism can act as a catalyst for a renewed appreciation of literature and its power to shape our understanding of the world.

Influence on reading habits and literature consumption

Digital minimalism has a profound influence on reading habits and literature consumption in today's society. By disconnecting from the constant distractions of digital devices, individuals are able to carve out more time for deep reading and meaningful engagement with literature. This intentional focus on quality reading material allows for a more enriching and immersive experience, fostering a deeper appreciation for the written word. As individuals prioritize the value of literature in their lives, they may find themselves drawn to diverse genres and authors, expanding their literary horizons and broadening their intellectual perspectives. Through digital minimalism, individuals can cultivate a more intentional and mindful approach to reading, leading to a greater appreciation for the transformative power of literature in their lives. Ultimately, by disconnecting from digital noise, individuals can reconnect with the timeless beauty and depth of literature, enhancing their overall well-being and intellectual growth.

Literary movements inspired by digital minimalism

One literary movement inspired by digital minimalism is the rise of "slow reading." While technology has made information more accessible than ever, it has also led to shorter attention spans and a culture of distraction. Slow reading advocates for a return to deep, focused reading by disconnecting from digital devices and immersing oneself in a single text. This movement encourages readers to savor the experience of reading, allowing for a more profound understanding and connection with the material. By engaging in slow reading practices, individuals can cultivate critical thinking skills, improve their ability to concentrate, and enhance their overall sense of well-being. In a world saturated with constant stimulation, slow reading offers a much-needed antidote by fostering mindfulness and intentionality in the reading process. This literary movement exemplifies how embracing digital minimalism can lead to a more enriching and meaningful relationship with literature.

Prominent authors and works discussing digital minimalism

Numerous prominent authors have contributed to the discourse surrounding digital minimalism. Cal Newport's book "Digital

Minimalism: Choosing a Focused Life in a Noisy World" has gained considerable popularity for its insightful approach to reducing digital distractions and reclaiming control over one's attention. Newport advocates for a deliberate and intentional use of technology to enhance one's well-being, rather than allowing it to dictate one's life. Additionally, Jaron Lanier's "Ten Arguments for Deleting Your Social Media Accounts Right Now" offers a critical examination of the negative impact of social media on mental health and social interactions. Lanier argues that digital platforms often exploit users' attention for profit, leading to a loss of autonomy and genuine human connection. These works highlight the importance of conscious and mindful engagement with technology in the modern age, encouraging readers to prioritize real-life experiences over digital distractions.

XLVI. DIGITAL MINIMALISM AND MUSIC

In the realm of digital minimalism, the impact of music consumption cannot be overlooked. As technology continues to advance, individuals have access to an overwhelming amount of music at their fingertips. This abundance can lead to a sense of information overload, making it challenging for individuals to truly appreciate and engage with the music they encounter. By practicing digital minimalism in their music consumption habits, individuals can cultivate a more intentional and focused listening experience. This may involve curating a select playlist of meaningful songs, savoring albums in their entirety without distractions, or even opting for analog methods of listening to music. By reducing the noise and clutter that often accompany digital music platforms, individuals can better connect with the music they love and derive greater enjoyment and fulfillment from their listening experiences.

Changes in music consumption and production

As technology continues to evolve, the landscape of music consumption and production has undergone significant changes. The advent of streaming services has revolutionized how people access and listen to music, with platforms like Spotify and Apple Music dominating the market. This shift towards digital formats has not only democratized access to music but has also transformed the way artists create and distribute their work. Independent musicians now have the ability to reach a global audience without the need for traditional record labels, bypassing traditional gatekeepers in the industry. The rise of social media and online platforms has also enabled artists to engage directly with their fans, cultivating a more intimate and interactive relationship. These developments have reshaped the music industry, challenging established norms and opening up new opportunities for both artists and listeners alike.

Musicians and composers adopting digital minimalism

In today's digital age, musicians and composers are embracing the principles of digital minimalism to streamline their creative processes and enhance productivity. By adopting a minimalist approach to their digital tools and devices, these artists are able to eliminate distractions and focus more intently on their craft. Rather than being overwhelmed by the constant influx of notifications and information, musicians are utilizing minimalist apps and software to simplify their workflows and enhance their creative output. This intentional curation of digital tools not only allows for a more efficient creative process but also fosters a deeper connection to the music being created. Through digital minimalism, musicians and composers are reclaiming control over their creative spaces and finding a better balance between technology and artistic expression. This shift towards a more intentional use of digital tools is revolutionizing the way music is being created and shared in today's fast-paced world.

Impact on the music industry

Digital minimalism has had a significant impact on the music industry, particularly in how artists create and distribute their music. With the rise of streaming services and social media platforms, musicians have found new ways to connect with their audience and promote their work. By embracing a minimalist approach to their online presence, artists can focus on creating high-quality music without being distracted by the pressures of maintaining a constant digital presence. This shift towards digital minimalism has also changed the way music is consumed, with listeners having access to a vast library of music at their fingertips. While this accessibility has its benefits, it has also posed challenges for artists to stand out in a crowded digital landscape. Overall, the influence of digital minimalism on the music industry highlights the need for artists to find a balance between utilizing technology to reach their audience and preserving the integrity of their artistry.

XLVII. DIGITAL MINIMALISM AND SPORTS

In the realm of sports, digital minimalism offers a refreshing approach to optimizing performance and focus. Athletes who adopt a minimalist mindset can harness the power of technology without being consumed by it. By reducing distractions and streamlining their digital lives, athletes can enhance their mindfulness and mental clarity, leading to improved decision-making on and off the field. Moreover, digital minimalism can help athletes build stronger connections with teammates and coaches by fostering more meaningful face-to-face interactions. In a world where technology dominates every aspect of our lives, embracing digital minimalism in sports can be a game-changer. It allows athletes to unplug from the constant barrage of notifications and alerts, enabling them to fully immerse themselves in their training and competitions. Ultimately, digital minimalism in sports offers a pathway to greater performance, resilience, and well-being.

Influence on sports training and viewing

The rise of digital technology has significantly impacted sports training and viewing experiences. Athletes now have access to a wealth of data and analysis tools that can help them optimize their performance and tailor their training regimens to their specific needs. Coaches can use digital platforms to track progress, set goals, and provide personalized feedback to their athletes remotely. Furthermore, fans can now engage with sports in ways never before possible, from live streaming games to participating in online fantasy leagues. With social media platforms enabling real-time updates and interactive discussions, the digital landscape has transformed the way we consume and interact with sports. However, while digital advancements have brought many benefits, they have also raised concerns about the potential for distraction and addiction. Finding a balance between leveraging technology for improved training and viewing experiences while not succumbing to its detrimental effects is key in the age of digital minimalism.

Sports organizations adopting minimal digital strategies

In the realm of sports organizations, the adoption of minimal digital strategies can present both challenges and benefits. While many may argue that a strong online presence is essential for engaging fans and promoting events, some organizations have found success in taking a more minimalist approach. By focusing on quality over quantity, these sports entities can create a more meaningful connection with their audience. Through strategic use of social media platforms, email marketing, and targeted advertising, sports organizations can cut through the digital noise and deliver content that is relevant and engaging. This targeted approach allows for a more personalized experience for fans, leading to increased loyalty and engagement. By embracing digital minimalism, sports organizations can create a streamlined and effective online presence that enhances the overall fan experience without overwhelming them with constant updates and information.

Athlete experiences with digital minimalism

Athletes have been increasingly turning to digital minimalism as a way to enhance their performance and focus on their craft. By reducing screen time and limiting distractions from social media and other digital platforms, athletes can devote more time to training, recovery, and mental preparation. In a world where technology permeates every aspect of life, disconnecting can be a powerful tool for improving athletic performance. By engaging in digital minimalism, athletes can cultivate a deeper connection with their sport, increase their ability to concentrate, and ultimately achieve better results. This shift towards a more intentional and focused use of technology has the potential to revolutionize the way athletes approach their training and competition, leading to improved outcomes and a more balanced, fulfilling athletic experience.

XLVIII. DIGITAL MINIMALISM AND VOLUNTEERING

In the context of digital minimalism, volunteering can offer a refreshing break from the constant presence of technology in our lives. By engaging in meaningful volunteer work, individuals can disconnect from their devices and connect with their communities on a deeper level. Volunteering provides a sense of purpose and fulfillment that is often lacking in the digital world, allowing individuals to make a tangible impact in the lives of others. This hands-on approach to giving back not only benefits the community but also promotes personal growth and self-reflection. Through volunteering, individuals can shift their focus away from the digital realm and towards real-world interactions, fostering a sense of empathy, compassion, and solidarity. By incorporating volunteering into a digital minimalist lifestyle, individuals can strike a balance between engaging with technology and nurturing meaningful relationships and experiences offline.

Volunteering in a minimally digital context

In today's society, where technology dominates almost every aspect of our lives, the concept of volunteering in a minimally digital context can offer a refreshing escape from the constant barrage of notifications and screen time. Engaging in volunteer work without relying heavily on digital tools can provide a sense of groundedness and connection to the community in a more tangible way. By focusing on direct human interactions and hands-on activities, individuals can experience a deeper level of fulfillment and satisfaction that may be lacking in the digital realm. Additionally, volunteering in a minimally digital context allows individuals to cultivate essential skills such as communication, empathy, and problem-solving without the distractions of technology. This approach to volunteering not only benefits the community but also offers individuals a much-needed break from the digital noise, fostering a more balanced and meaningful existence.

Promoting community service without digital overload

In today's society, where digital technologies dominate our daily lives and interactions, it can be challenging to promote community service without succumbing to digital overload. One effective way to address this issue is to emphasize the importance of offline connections and face-to-face interactions. By focusing on building relationships in the real world, individuals can engage with their communities in a more meaningful and impactful way. Encouraging people to volunteer in person, attend local events, and participate in community projects can foster a sense of belonging and connection that goes beyond the superficial interactions often found online. It is essential to create opportunities for individuals to unplug from their devices and engage with their surroundings actively. By striking a balance between digital engagement and real-world experiences, we can promote community service without being overwhelmed by the digital noise that often pervades our lives.

Case studies of volunteering initiatives

In examining case studies of volunteering initiatives, we can gain valuable insight into the impact of community engagement and the benefits it brings to both the volunteers and the recipients of their service. For example, a study on a local food bank volunteer program may reveal how individuals experienced increased feelings of fulfillment and satisfaction from helping those in need, while also forming stronger social connections with fellow volunteers. These case studies can also shed light on the effectiveness of different approaches to recruitment, training, and retention of volunteers, providing valuable lessons for organizations seeking to expand their volunteer base. By analyzing the outcomes of various volunteering initiatives, we can not only appreciate the positive effects of giving back to the community but also identify best practices for maximizing the impact of volunteer efforts in improving society as a whole.

XLIX. DIGITAL MINIMALISM AND HOBBIES

In today's technology-driven world, the concept of digital minimalism has gained popularity as individuals seek strategies to disconnect from the constant noise of digital devices. Central to this movement is the idea of reclaiming time and mental space by prioritizing meaningful real-world activities, such as hobbies. By embracing digital minimalism, individuals can dedicate more time to hobbies that bring joy, fulfillment, and a sense of accomplishment. For example, instead of mindlessly scrolling through social media feeds during free time, one can immerse themselves in activities like painting, gardening, or playing a musical instrument. These hobbies not only provide a much-needed break from screen time but also offer tangible benefits such as stress relief, improved focus, and a boost in creativity. Ultimately, incorporating hobbies into a digital minimalist lifestyle can lead to a more balanced and enriched existence.

Rediscovering and promoting traditional hobbies

Rediscovering and promoting traditional hobbies can serve as a powerful antidote to the incessant digital distractions that pervade our modern lives. Engaging in activities like woodworking, gardening, or painting allows individuals to step away from screens and reconnect with the tangible world around them. These hobbies offer a sense of fulfillment that is often lacking in the virtual realm, providing opportunities for creativity, skill development, and stress relief. By embracing traditional pastimes, individuals can cultivate a sense of mindfulness and presence that is vital for mental well-being. Furthermore, these activities provide a much-needed break from the constant stream of information and stimulation that technology inundates us with. In rediscovering traditional hobbies, individuals can find a sense of balance and harmony in their lives, ultimately leading to a more fulfilling and enriching existence.

Community groups focused on non-digital hobbies

As individuals seek ways to disconnect from the overwhelming digital world around them, community groups focused on non-digital hobbies offer a refreshing alternative. These groups provide a space for like-minded individuals to come together and engage in activities that do not involve screens or technology. Whether it's a book club, gardening group, or woodworking workshop, these gatherings promote face-to-face interactions, creativity, and a sense of belonging. By participating in non-digital hobbies within a community setting, individuals can enjoy a break from the constant barrage of notifications and distractions from their devices. These groups not only offer a chance to learn new skills or pursue long-standing interests but also foster meaningful connections with others who share similar passions. In a world where digital devices dominate our daily lives, community groups focused on non-digital hobbies serve as a valuable tool for promoting mindfulness, fulfillment, and a much-needed break from the digital noise.

Personal stories of hobbyists

Within the realm of digital minimalism, personal stories of hobbyists offer valuable insights into the benefits of disconnecting from technology. When hobbyists share their experiences of reducing screen time and engaging in offline activities, it becomes evident that the quality of their lives improves significantly. These individuals often report feeling more present, creative, and fulfilled when they spend less time in front of screens and more time pursuing hobbies that bring them joy. For some, it may be woodworking, painting, or gardening, while others find solace in cooking, reading, or playing musical instruments. By prioritizing these analog activities over digital distractions, hobbyists are able to cultivate deeper connections with themselves and those around them. Through their stories, it becomes clear that embracing digital minimalism can lead to a more balanced and meaningful existence.

L. REVIEW AND FUTURE DIRECTIONS

In the final section of the book, Newport delves into the review of his concept of digital minimalism and offers insights into potential future directions for individuals seeking to adopt this lifestyle. By reflecting on the principles and strategies outlined throughout the book, readers are encouraged to assess their own habits and make necessary adjustments to prioritize real-world experiences over digital distractions. Newport emphasizes the importance of regularly evaluating one's relationship with technology and remaining open to evolving practices that align with personal values and goals. Looking ahead, the author suggests that the digital minimalism movement will continue to gain momentum as more people recognize the benefits of intentional technology use. This section serves as a call to action, challenging readers to embrace a more mindful approach to their digital lives and paving the way for a future where technology enriches rather than consumes our daily existence.

Summary of key findings and themes

In examining the key findings and themes of digital minimalism, it becomes evident that the practice offers a solution to the pervasive issue of technology addiction in modern society. By intentionally reducing the time spent on digital devices and focusing on meaningful, offline activities, individuals can reclaim their autonomy and mental well-being. One of the central themes that emerges is the importance of establishing boundaries with technology to prevent its encroachment on personal interactions and mental health. Additionally, digital minimalism emphasizes the value of deep work and focused attention, leading to increased productivity and creativity. Through implementing strategies such as decluttering digital spaces and engaging in solitude, individuals can cultivate a more intentional and purposeful approach to technology use. Overall, the findings point towards the transformative potential of digital minimalism in restoring balance and mindfulness in an increasingly connected world.

Recommendations for further research and practice

In light of the findings presented in this essay, there are several recommendations for further research and practice in the realm of digital minimalism. Firstly, future research could delve into the impact of digital minimalism on mental health outcomes such as stress, anxiety, and overall well-being. Understanding the psychological benefits of disconnecting from technology could provide valuable insights for individuals and mental health professionals alike. Additionally, exploring the effects of digital minimalism on productivity and creativity could offer practical strategies for individuals looking to optimize their work and personal lives. Finally, further research could investigate the long-term effects of sustained digital minimalism practices on forming healthy habits and sustaining behavior change. By addressing these areas of inquiry, researchers and practitioners can continue to advance our understanding of digital minimalism and its potential benefits for promoting a healthier and more balanced lifestyle.

Final thoughts on the sustainability of digital minimalism

In conclusion, the sustainability of digital minimalism lies in its ability to cultivate a mindful and intentional approach to technology use. By decluttering our digital spaces and setting clear boundaries, individuals can regain control over their time and attention, leading to improved mental well-being and a more balanced lifestyle. However, the success of digital minimalism ultimately depends on individual commitment and discipline. It requires a conscious effort to resist the constant pull of notifications, social media, and other digital distractions. While digital minimalism offers a promising solution to the negative impact of excessive screen time, it is not a one-size-fits-all approach. Each person must find their own balance and adapt the principles of digital minimalism to suit their unique needs and priorities. Overall, embracing digital minimalism can lead to a more fulfilling and purposeful existence in today's hyper-connected world.

LI. CONCLUSION

In conclusion, the concept of digital minimalism offers a compelling solution to the overwhelming presence of technology in our lives. By disconnecting from the constant barrage of notifications, emails, and social media, individuals can reclaim their time and attention for more meaningful pursuits. Through intentional curation of digital tools and platforms, one can create a digital environment that aligns with their values and goals. This process requires reflection, discipline, and a willingness to challenge societal norms around technology use. Ultimately, the practice of digital minimalism can lead to greater focus, creativity, and overall well-being. As we navigate an increasingly connected world, embracing a minimalist approach to our digital lives may be the key to striking a balance between the benefits of technology and the need for solitude and presence. By prioritizing quality over quantity in our digital interactions, we can cultivate a more fulfilling and purposeful existence.

Recapitulation of the importance of digital minimalism

In today's hyper-connected world, the importance of digital minimalism cannot be overstated. By intentionally limiting our time spent on digital devices and social media platforms, we can reclaim control over our attention and focus on what truly matters. Digital minimalism allows us to cultivate deep and meaningful relationships, engage in mindfulness practices, and prioritize our mental health and well-being. Through disconnecting from the constant barrage of notifications and distractions, we can create space for creativity, critical thinking, and self-reflection. Embracing a minimalist approach to technology not only enhances our daily productivity but also fosters a sense of balance and harmony in our lives. By practicing digital minimalism, we can unlock a more intentional and fulfilling existence, free from the overwhelming demands of the digital world.

Final reflections on personal and societal benefits

Throughout this exploration of digital minimalism, it has become apparent that the benefits extend beyond just personal well-being to societal advantages as well. By disconnecting from the constant barrage of digital distractions, individuals are able to cultivate deeper relationships with those around them, fostering a more connected and empathetic community. Additionally, a reduction in screen time allows for increased focus and productivity, leading to enhanced performance in both personal and professional endeavors. Furthermore, as individuals prioritize real-life experiences over virtual ones, they contribute to the creation of a healthier and more balanced society. Ultimately, by embracing digital minimalism, individuals not only improve their own mental health and well-being but also contribute positively to the collective societal fabric, creating a more meaningful and fulfilling existence for themselves and those around them.

Call to action for embracing a digitally minimalist lifestyle

In a society where technology dominates nearly every aspect of daily life, it is essential to consider adopting a digitally minimalist lifestyle to combat the overwhelming presence of digital distractions. Embracing digital minimalism involves intentionally evaluating the role technology plays in our lives and making conscious choices to prioritize meaningful activities over mindless scrolling. By reducing screen time and focusing on real-world interactions, individuals can reclaim their time and mental space for pursuits that truly bring fulfillment and satisfaction. This shift towards a minimalist approach can lead to increased productivity, improved mental well-being, and deeper connections with others. With a deliberate call to action for embracing digital minimalism, individuals can cultivate a healthier relationship with technology and create a more balanced and fulfilling life. By taking control of our digital habits, we can pave the way for a more intentional and purposeful existence in today's fast-paced and technology-driven world.

BIBLIOGRAPHY

Robert East. 'The Effect of Advertising and Display.' Assessing the Evidence, Springer Science & Business Media, 3/20/2013

Paul C. Adams. 'Disentangling.' The Geographies of Digital Disconnection, André Jansson, Oxford University Press, 1/1/2021

Emma L. Slade. 'Digital and Social Media Marketing.' Emerging Applications and Theoretical Development, Nripendra P. Rana, Springer Nature, 11/11/2019

Kam Knight. 'Speed Reading.' Learn to Read a 200+ Page Book in 1 Hour, Amazon Digital Services LLC - Kdp, 9/26/2018

Introbooks. 'Digital Minimalism.' Independently Published, 1/21/2020

Division on Engineering and Physical Sciences. 'Energy-Efficiency Standards and Green Building Certification Systems Used by the Department of Defense for Military Construction and Major Renovations.' National Research Council, National Academies Press, 6/4/2013

Stephanie Marie Seferian. 'Sustainable Minimalism.' Embrace Zero Waste, Build Sustainability Habits That Last, and Become a Minimalist Without Sacrificing the Planet, Mango Media Inc., 1/19/2021

Stephen M. Testa. 'Environmental Considerations Associated with Hydraulic Fracturing Operations.' Adjusting to the Shale Revolution in a Green World, James A. Jacobs, John Wiley & Sons, 4/23/2019

Steve Case. 'The Third Wave.' An Entrepreneur's Vision of the Future, Simon and Schuster, 4/18/2017

Zenia Z. Kotval. 'Financing Economic Development in the 21st Century.' Sammis B. White, Routledge, 12/18/2014

Irene Papanicolas. 'Health System Efficiency.' How to Make Measurement Matter for Policy and Management, World Health Organization, 12/15/2016

Patricia Connelly. 'Theoretical Perspectives on Gender and Development.' Jane L. Parpart, IDRC, 1/1/2000

Swasti Mitter. 'Gender and the Digital Economy.' Perspectives From the Developing World, Cecilia Ng, SAGE, 11/5/2005

Rebekah Willett. 'Digital Generations.' Children, Young People, and the New Media, David Buckingham, Routledge, 10/18/2013

S. Shigetomi. 'Protest and Social Movements in the Developing World.' Edward Elgar Publishing, 1/1/2009

Felix B. Tan. 'Advanced Topics in Global Information Management.' Idea Group Inc (IGI), 1/1/2002

Chaudhary, Shilpa. 'Business Drivers in Promoting Digital Detoxification.' Grima, Simon, IGI Global, 1/10/2024

Susan Elswick. 'Data Collection.' Methods, Ethical Issues and Future Directions, Nova Publishers, Incorporated, 1/1/2017

George D. Pozgar. 'Legal and Ethical Issues for Health Professionals.' Jones & Bartlett Learning, 1/7/2019

Katie Shilton. 'Business and the Ethical Implications of Technology.' Kirsten Martin, Springer Nature, 11/9/2022

Elin M. Oftedal. 'Responsible Innovation in Digital Health.' Empowering the Patient, Tatiana Iakovleva, Edward Elgar Publishing, 1/1/2019

Asher Flynn. 'The Emerald International Handbook of Technology-Facilitated Violence and Abuse.' Jane Bailey, Emerald Group Publishing, 6/4/2021

Tanya Dalton. 'The Joy of Missing Out.' Live More by Doing Less, Thomas Nelson, 10/1/2019

Sherah Kurnia. 'Social Inclusion and Usability of ICT-enabled Services..' Jyoti Choudrie, Routledge, 10/31/2017

John Townsend. 'Boundaries.' When to Say Yes, How to Say No, to Take Control of Your Life, Henry Cloud, Zondervan, 3/18/2002

Tiziano Vescovi. *'Managing Digital Transformation.'* Understanding the Strategic Process, Andreas Hinterhuber, Routledge, 5/26/2021

Gupta, Brij B.. *'Handbook of Research on Digital Transformation Management and Tools.'* Pettinger, Richard, IGI Global, 6/30/2022

Mark Taylor. *'Digital Minimalism.'* 17 Books Publishing, 12/2/2018

Michael Bunting. *'The Mindful Leader.'* 7 Practices for Transforming Your Leadership, Your Organisation and Your Life, John Wiley & Sons, 8/22/2016

Harvard Business Review. *'Fostering Creativity.'* Harvard Business Press, 3/1/2010

Amy Jo Kim. *'Community Building on the Web.'* Secret Strategies for Successful Online Communities, Peachpit Press, 7/19/2006

Dr. Barry J. Hammer. *'Deepening Your Personal Relationships.'* Developing Emotional Intimacy and Good Communication, Dr. Max Hammer, Strategic Book Publishing, 12/1/2013

Arthur Martin Cohen. *'The Effects of Changes in Patterns of Communication on the Behaviors of Problem-solving Groups.'* Boston University, 1/1/1959

James Hiebert. *'Teachers, Teaching, and Reform.'* Perspectives on Efforts to Improve Educational Outcomes, Ralph P. Ferretti, Routledge, 12/14/2017

Dan Gaines. *'How to Be a Digital Minimalist.'* Simplify Your Life and Eliminate Clutter Using Technology, Lulu Press, Incorporated, 8/31/2019

Food and Nutrition Board. *'Educating the Student Body.'* Taking Physical Activity and Physical Education to School, Committee on Physical Activity and Physical Education in the School Environment, National Academies Press, 11/13/2013

David Rust. *'Sorry, I Have to Take This.'* Breaking Free from Digital Distractions, CreateSpace Independent Publishing Platform, 1/22/2014

James J. Jaurez. *'Increasing Productivity and Efficiency in Online Teaching.'* Patricia Dickenson, IGI Global, 1/1/2016

Division of Behavioral and Social Sciences and Education. 'Social Isolation and Loneliness in Older Adults.' Opportunities for the Health Care System, National Academies of Sciences, Engineering, and Medicine, National Academies Press, 5/14/2020

Wes Burgess. 'Calm Your Mind.' Exercises to Reduce Stress, Improve Focus, and Control Anxiety, Anger, and Depression, CreateSpace Independent Publishing Platform, 7/29/2011

Mary Beth Oliver. 'The Routledge Handbook of Media Use and Well-Being.' International Perspectives on Theory and Research on Positive Media Effects, Leonard Reinecke, Routledge, 6/23/2016

G. Underwood. 'Attention and Memory.' Elsevier, 10/22/2013

Carol Saunders. 'Emotional and Cognitive Overload.' The Dark Side of Information Technology, Anne-Françoise Rutkowski, Routledge, 10/3/2018

Brian D. Loader. 'Routledge Handbook of Digital Media and Communication.' Leah A. Lievrouw, Routledge, 11/16/2020

Katherine Ormerod. 'Why Social Media is Ruining Your Life.' Octopus, 9/10/2018

Leora Klapper. 'The Global Findex Database 2017.' Measuring Financial Inclusion and the Fintech Revolution, Asli Demirguc-Kunt, World Bank Publications, 4/19/2018

Daniel Jackson. 'Digital Detox and Digital Minimalism.' Rockwood Publishing, 10/31/2023

Susan Carey. 'The Origin of Concepts.' Oxford University Press, 1/1/2011

Lucile Vaughan Payne. 'The Lively Art of Writing.' Words, Sentences, Style and Technique -- an Essential Guide to One of Today's Most Necessary Skills, Penguin, 3/1/1969

Alexander Cooper. 'Summary of Digital Minimalism.' by Cal Newport - Choosing a Focused Life in a Noisy World - A Comprehensive Summary, BookSummaryGr, 10/3/2021

Cal Newport. 'Digital Minimalism.' Choosing a Focused Life in a Noisy World, Penguin, 2/5/2019

Alistair McCleery. 'An Introduction to Book History.' David Finkelstein, Routledge, 3/13/2006